Moving to France
with your children

Moving to France

new language · making friends · what's what · who's who · tests · teaching style · option choices · career paths · finding help · school meals · food · sport · school life · parenting · life-style · mother tongue · culture · making friends · reading · new language · making friends · what's what · who's who · tests · teaching style · option choices · career paths · finding help · school meals · food · sport · school life · parenting · life-style · mother tongue · culture · making friends · reading · new language · making friends · what's what · who's who · tests · teaching style · option choices · career paths · finding help · school meals · food · sport · school life · parenting · life-style · mother tongue · culture · making friends

with your children

ANGIE POWER

howto**books**

... at *The Daily Telegraph* for publishing my first article on education in France since it gave me a chance to recount my experiences, in the hope of helping other parents find their way around their children's newly adopted school system.

I am grateful to Lisbeth Wille for the photographs.

Published by How To Books Ltd,
Spring Hill House, Spring Hill Road,
Begbroke, Oxford OX5 1RX, United Kingdom
Tel: (01865) 375794 Fax: (01865) 379162
email: info@howtobooks.co.uk
http://www.howtobooks.co.uk

The right of Angie Power to be identified as author of this work has been asserted by her in accordance with the Copyright, Design and Patents Act 1988.

British Library Cataloguing in Publication Data
A catalogue record for this book is available from
the British Library.

First published 2007

ISBN: 978 1 84528 166 3

Photo Gallery: © Lisbeth Wille
Produced for How To Books by Deer Park Productions, Tavistock
Typeset by *specialist* publishing services ltd, Montgomery
Printed and bound by Bell and Bain Ltd, Glasgow

NOTE: The material contained in this book is set out in good faith for general guidance and no liability can be accepted for loss or expense incurred as a result of relying in particular circumstances on statements made in the book. The laws and regulations are complex and liable to change, and readers should check the current with the relevant authorities before taking action.

Contents

Preface

Moving to France with your children is a collection of reflections and helpful advice based on my own experiences as both an English parent and a teacher living in a small French town.

The book attempts to enlighten newly arrived – and established – families on unfamiliar but fascinating matters which need to be considered by parents wishing their children to be comfortable and to succeed in their new environment. Above all, it aims to be reassuring and inspirational to families who want to enhance their children's integration into French life.

The chapters cover various aspects of French culture and school life and have been grouped together into three sections. The first section – *An adjustment for the whole family* – looks at how parents themselves need to feel at ease in their new surroundings. on the one hand communicating in French at work and with friends and neighbours, whilst on the other hand maintaining their children's English language and culture at home.

The second section – *Education and learning* – helps parents find their way around their children's new school system so that they may make the most of the opportunities available.

The third and final section – *The Appeal of the French lifestyle for young and old alike* – reveals traditions, past-times and festivities an occasional tourist might miss, reminding us of why we moved to France in the first place!

Moving to France with your children took as long to write as it took my children to complete their schooling here. I can clearly remember the conversation – about ten years ago, when my sons were both at primary school – and an English visitor first expressed the idea that there were probably other parents who might want to share my observations. He had been listening to a typical school day of ours; of how one son had had to stand on the teacher's platform in the morning and recite all the rivers in France to the whole class and how my other son had to learn the national anthem by heart for the next day. Neither boy had been punished: this was everyday school work and typical of the tough, rigorous school system for which many English families are unprepared. True, our conversation verged on the humorous because I explained how I had forgotten the tune of *La Marseillaise* and we had had to ask our 80-year-old neighbour whose out-of-tune rendition of it was simply unforgettable. Nevertheless, the Englishman was so serious about my writing that he suggested a list of newspaper editors to whom I might write. So it is – many published articles later and with yet more to share – that a book for other parents moving to France with their children has finally come about.

Angie Power

Take more of your money with you

If you're planning a move to the France it's likely that the last thing on your mind is foreign exchange. However, at some point you will have to change your hard earned money into euros. Unfortunately, exchange rates are constantly moving and as a result can have a big impact on the amount of money you have to create your dream home.

For example, if you look at the euro during 2005 you can see how this movement can affect your capital. Sterling against the euro was as high as 1.5124 and as low as 1.4086. This meant that if you had £200,000 you could have ended up with as much as €302,480 or as little as €281,720, a difference of over €20,000.

It is possible to avoid this pitfall by fixing a rate through a **forward contract**. A small deposit will secure you a rate for anywhere up to 2 years in advance and by doing so provides the security of having the currency you need at a guaranteed cost.

Another option if you have time on your side is a **limit order**. This is used when you want to achieve a rate that is currently not available. You set the rate that you want and the market is then monitored. As soon as that rate is achieved the currency is purchased for you.

If you need to act swiftly and your capital is readily available then it is most likely that you will use a **spot transaction**. This is the *Buy now, Pay now* option where you get the most competitive rate on the day.

To ensure you get the most for you money it's a good idea to use a foreign exchange specialist such as Currencies Direct. As an alternative to your bank, Currencies Direct is able to offer you extremely competitive exchange rates, no commission charges and free transfers*. This can mean considerable savings on your transfer when compared to using a bank.

*Over £5,000

Information provided by Currencies Direct.
Website: *www.currenciesdirect.com*
Email: *info@currenciesdirect.com*
Tel: 0845 389 1729

An adjustment for the whole family

1
Foreigners in a French land

Over 20 years ago, my husband and I moved from the UK to live in a small provincial town in France. I did not realise that life was going to be so unlike the city lifestyle I was used to in Britain – after all France is not so far away. But it was when we had our children and we were bringing them up that we became more fully aware of the differences in culture and the way of doing things.

FRENCH RED TAPE

It took me some time to get used to the ever-present and long-winded French bureaucracy. I left England with my passport and my driving licence. Little did I know that once I had decided to reside in France I would need the same wallet-full of documents that the French have. It was a nightmare because certain documents can only be issued if you were born or married in France.

Even to this day, there is a look of disbelief when a *livret de famille* is required and I say I have not got one. Details about

3

your children's births are recorded in this booklet and in some situations it is the required proof that you are a family: for example, we were once unable to get a reduction on a family pass for the ski slopes because we did not have a *livret de famille*.

I clearly remember civil servants laughing when I said that I did not have an identity card: they laughed even louder when I tried to explain that where I come from we do not need one. When I showed them my driving licence, they positively howled: they could not believe it was valid because there was no photograph attached. They replaced it – at a cost for administrative charges – with a French driving licence. A photo of me is attached *bien sûr*!

Nowadays, I no longer moan at red tape because so many French people themselves find it frustrating. They justify it by saying that there is a whole army of civil servants – I have seen figures referring to 1.9 million of them and others referring to as many as one in five of all those employed – who need to be occupied and paid. The issuing and renewal of documents do just that. Seeing it in these terms – keeping your fellow citizen in employment – makes all that time (and money) you spend a little easier to accept.

PROOF OF IDENTITY

The French believe strongly in checking people's identity. If you write a cheque in a supermarket for example, the cashier will ask you for your identity card to guarantee the authenticity of the cheque. At first, this offended my sense of privacy. Proof is required every time, too. I have been unable to claim parcels at the Post Office because I have presumed that they now know me. The simplest thing is to always carry the documents with you, like everyone else. Is that why some French men carry those little handbags – I ask myself – because all their *papiers* will not fit into their pockets!

THE FRENCH APPROACH

Things are done differently here. I was quite shocked the first time I visited a GP and he himself asked me for a cheque at the end of the consultation. The handing over of money to people in the medical profession feels wrong at first: surely, I thought, they are above collecting cheques. Nowadays, most people hand over their *carte vital* too, in order to speed up the reimbursement process. I have had to accept their way of doing things: you just cannot leave the surgery without settling up. Like others in the service industry, they provide what you need and you pay.

Another problem I had was shaking people's hands so often. I felt uncomfortable touching, and anxious about passing germs, but living in another country means looking at things from a local's viewpoint. It is their way of acknowledging your presence.

THE LANGUAGE GAP

The language was an enormous handicap because when I arrived, I could only speak a few words. Even following directions on boxes of food was difficult! However, I found a French teacher and I made rapid progress during the first few years. She explained everything to me in English although some people at the time said that since I was now living in France my teacher should only have spoken French to me. I would not have followed had she only spoken in French, leaving it up to me to guess the grammar rules and subtleties of the vocabulary.

Even after living here for so long, though, I still sound like a foreigner. As with many adults learning a new language, I have now reached a 'plateau': progress is slow. I avoid arguments because I cannot express myself, I often miss out on a joke and I have to have my children to check the notes I send with them to school for mistakes. But I would not call it a language barrier now because I can follow conversations without struggling too much.

THE GOOD LIFE

At some point, the annoying aspects of French life have faded into the background. My struggle to master the language and the domineering bureaucracy still exist and I know that I will always have to wait for months for some local tradesmen. But the longer I have lived here the more my lifestyle and that of my family, has improved.

Food is important to the French and, nowadays, for me too. The French are concerned about freshness. Watch them chose the ripest melons or the way they run their fingers along a *camembert*. Given the chance, they go out into the forests or fields to collect their snails, mushrooms and berries. They even prefer using *sarment* (the small shoots that are pruned from the vines) rather than charcoal for their barbecues because it gives a better flavour. It is hard not to become a food or wine buff.

Above all, mealtime has a social importance. The whole extended family gets together for bank holidays. Evenings are spent with friends around the table. Village life means you are only a walk away from home and you do not need to drive.

I like the element of choice that is available. If I do not want to pay a road toll and I am not in any hurry, then I use the *route nationale*. If I do not want the inconvenience of too many trucks, then I take the motorway and I pay the toll. In the same way, I get a choice of doctor and dentist that I prefer and I can usually get to see them when I want – that is to say, without too long a wait. I can contribute to the school life of my children if I choose because each class has two parent representatives.

BRINGING UP THE CHILDREN

Above all, the richest adventure for me has been that of bringing up my children here because the experience has made France feel like home to me. Listening to my children reciting poetry, memorising historical dates and geographic facts and viewing incidents from a different perspective through them, has given me a better understanding of French culture and their approach to life.

Moving abroad – even just across the Channel – is not the same as moving across the street. I have had days when I have been caught up in some misunderstanding or another and I have also had to do things that have not seemed logical to me at all. But not for one moment do I regret experiencing how different we all are and how much we can learn from each other. After all, *c'est la vie!*

2
Coping with a new language for an adult

One of the most daunting aspects of living abroad is getting to grips with another language – and moving with children means communicating effectively is even more necessary. Why do adults find it so difficult?

MEMORY LOSS

Language learning revolves around how well we remember things and children can do this much better than adults can. Those foreign athletes and politicians we see on the television who mesmerise us by speaking English fluently, probably started learning it at a very early age and have never looked back. Adults who were lucky enough to get the basic elementary rules of grammar at school but have never since practised, may find that it will come back to them – vaguely – once they are in the country. For those of us who did not 'do' a language at school though, words and rules seem to go in through one ear and out of the other. Even then, we often have to see a sentence written down on paper to make any sense of it.

SAYING IT CORRECTLY

Another problem is pronunciation. As with all things in life, the ability to 'hear' and mimic new words has not been distributed fairly. Hence some people say a word correctly the first time whilst some of us have to listen to it a number of times before it sinks in.

Adults are touchy about making mistakes and being corrected. We feel we are being criticised or attacked. Added to that, we are inhibited and feel embarrassed making these new shapes and noises with our mouths. It seems *so* much easier to let someone else speak English to us!

PERSEVERANCE

Adults often do not have the staying power or discipline to learn a foreign language – a baby learning to walk puts us to shame. He tumbles over endless times but he gets up for another go. Adults are easily discouraged. It can take years of study and practice to speak fluently. (Do we speak our own language all the time without making any mistakes?) The best policy is to try your hardest but do not set your goals too high. Accept that you cannot do everything as well as you would like to do. You should not expect to make constant progress either: beginners feel they are sailing along whilst it is difficult to break through the 'intermediate plateau'.

LESSONS

Mastering a language cannot be 'bought' as such. Language lessons with a teacher are only useful if an adult is motivated:

there is no waving of a magic wand or a secret switch that the teacher turns on. Worse, many of us have awful school memories of being force-fed irregular verbs and being told we will never be linguists. You will know when you are ready for lessons – and some people never need them.

When it does come to enrolling for a language course, the mistake that is often made is that a class is chosen because the hours (or price) suit best. Ask questions about the make-up of the group because you will not make much progress if the class is not homogeneous. Beginners feel they are holding back other, more proficient, members of the group – and this is often true! Objectives are important too: do you need the language for your work while the others just want a survival course?

Expensive sets of language CDs or cassettes are sometimes bought, too, in the mistaken belief that it is an instant way of learning a language. You may well be demotivated by the very idea of all the time required to work through them. Language is a living thing – it is about communication: you need a few experiences of looking at real-life people in the eye first. Buy the expensive kits later on, if you want, once you get going.

Tips

- Those who often make the most progress are those who have **set an objective** for themselves: the goal may be to have enough understanding for your child's parent-teacher evening, to manage in French at an interview or to impress your first set of friends or family who are coming over to visit.

- It is possible to get yourself up and running without formal lessons. Borrow clear, **well-written vocabulary books** from the library if you can. Start

---

with colourful word books aimed at young children learning French. Better still, find books with cassettes or CDs that you can listen to over and over again in the car or at home. Begin slowly, aiming at learning five new words or verbs a day. Write them down on a piece of paper to test yourself. Then gradually increase the number every day. Work yourself up to secondary school level books where you will see those first basic grammar rules and the easy tenses. At all costs, avoid books with complicated jargon.

- **Buy a dictionary.** Even better buy two. One larger, more detailed one to keep at home and another smaller one to carry around – make sure though that the print is not too small because you will want to read it easily. Look up words you do not know before you go out for an errand or pick up the phone.

- Do not expect the locals to understand you first time, but do not falter: it is perhaps because you are nervous that they have not heard you. **Speak up** with confidence. Give the person you are talking to time to answer too: my sons say I keep repeating myself and that is because I assume I have not been understood whereas, in fact, that split second silence is thinking time.

- If you are really determined about speaking a foreign language then you should **maximise your opportunities** of doing so. Go to the local market to force yourself into situations where you need to speak to people. Unlike the assistants in the supermarket, local stall holders depend on you going back to buy, so they have time for a chat in the hope of making a new client. Speak to elderly people: they have time to talk and give you the opportunity of improving your new language.

- Watch the local **television**: you may pick up some basics just watching the commercials.

11

- Buy the local **newspaper** from time to time. You will find some useful words just going through the small ads! Without making it an academic exercise, force yourself to look up the odd word you do not understand in your dictionary. Even copy it out a few times on a blank piece of paper to assimilate it.

For adults, language learning is a long, hard process and we must not expect too much of ourselves too quickly. Think of it in terms of brushing your teeth: if you are serious about this, it is something that you have to spend a bit of time on every day.

What is there left to say but *bonne chance*?

3
Making friends with the locals

My French friends in the provincial south west of France where I live, commented recently on the proliferation of estate agents in our small town and they felt that there are more Anglo-Saxons settling down here. They tell me that they can often spot *un anglais* miles away: apparently it is the socks, sandals and pale legs that are the give away signs! 'But how do you identify an Englishman from afar during the winter-time when they are wearing shoes and long trousers?' I inquired. The reply from these French natives was immediate: the newly-arrived Englishman has a bewildered expression on his face – he looks lost!

BLEAK WINTER DAYS

For those who arrive here in the summer and then find themselves in the same town a few months later, yes, I imagine they would look taken aback by the transformation of the surroundings. Our town undergoes nothing short of a metamorphosis in the winter months. One can easily picture the colourful bustle of the streets during July or August when many locals take the opportunity to sit in the sun in the town square to sip their *citron pressé*. The place is positively vibrant over the summer months. These are days of non-stop music and street entertainment during the many fêtes and festivals. Boutiques selling postcards, local pottery and even garlic spring up overnight to feed the demand of passing visitors. Once the evenings start to close in and the rain begins to fall however, these same shops disappear and the locals go straight home from work and shutter themselves inside. Just outside the town centre too, the vines look ravaged once the grapes have been harvested. The place that looks so welcoming in summer looks rather unfriendly and lonely during the rest of the year.

THE IMPORTANCE OF FAMILY

As far as my French friends are concerned the newly-arrived English wandering round town looking slightly dazed, earn both their sympathy and admiration. Sympathy because for the French, life is so tied up with the other family members – both the close and the extended family – that as far as they are concerned, life must be a hardship spent apart. My son's decision to pursue his post *baccalauréat* studies abroad, rather than continue them here in France, was met with surprise and disbelief by some since most young students of the same age come home for the weekend whenever they possibly can. One friend even reprimanded me for not going with my son, to settle him in and buy his pots and pans!

It is true that you can feel a little left out of things here during the *ponts* – or long bank holiday weekends – because many of them are based around the family and the extended family. One example is *Toussaint* or All Saints' Day on November 1st when families get together to place flowers on their family graves, followed by a long, drawn-out family lunch. Pentecost is the time of the year for family reunions too, when communions and confirmations take place, again followed by a huge meal.

CONTACT

These occasions are more than meals however. They are opportunities for contact and exchange between family members, and when my French friends express their sympathy for the foreigner abroad, it is because they know how difficult it must be to know how things work without the help and support of close ones. The French themselves are the first to admit to how frustrating their bureaucracy can be and how difficult their codes of behaviour must seem to outsiders. This explains why they would go so far as to admire those who have chosen to settle down around them. French mothers where I live tell me how amazed they are that English families are enrolling their children at the local schools: admiration because they themselves know how daunting option choices and decisions on which course of study and where to do it can be, especially without a helping hand.

It is no easy task making new friends and the French themselves settling into small provincial towns are faced with the same problem. One reason is that local people already have their family and friends from childhood to occupy their time. For those within driving distance from a university, cultural centre or international school where there exists an enthusiasm on both sides to get together, it may be easier.

DO NOT BE TOO PUSHY

As with all things in small town France – and meeting new people is no exception – there is a certain way of doing things and, when I first arrived, I made a number of *faux-pas*. One of them was that I was too forward and keen. I had been introduced to a woman who was my age and I felt that I wanted to get to know her better. Since she lived in the same *quartier*, I knocked at the door one day when I was passing by and although she let me in, I realised that I had done something wrong. I now know that I should have phoned first to arrange a call because it is only very close friends who 'pop in'.

I also made blunders phoning at the wrong time of the day because it is understood that there are certain times that one should and should not phone: never before ten o'clock in the morning whereas *l'heure du repas* (meal time) seems to be the most acceptable time.

FORGET THE CUPPA

When you live abroad, you take your own social codes and ways of behaviour with you and they are not always appropriate. Take our English habit of offering a drink to make visitors feel welcome at any time of the day. It breaks the ice when you have just met someone. However, I have been laughed at when I have offered a cup of coffee just before lunch time and I have had strange looks when I have suggested a glass of wine at six o'clock. For the French, these were both inappropriate times. On the other hand, whereas I feel uncomfortable standing around, my French friends will quite happily chat in a supermarket or on the way back from school if they want to talk to me.

SPOT THE OCCASION

The opportunities for meeting new people are difficult to recognise at first. There is no local pub and, in my town at least, it would not be the done thing for a group of married girlfriends to meet once a week in the evening at the local bar. School events are hardly the occasion for parents to meet socially either, because there are so few fund-raising events. Parents even at state primary schools are asked to make a fixed 'contribution' to help pay for extras. True, our local primary school traditionally throws an annual bingo session but – let's face it – holding a conversation with someone shouting out numbers in the background, is hardly an ideal place for meeting new friends! Even when your child throws a birthday party, parents drop their children off and tend not to want to come in because they 'don't know you'. At the workplace, colleagues may have a quiet glass of champagne over a *Galette des Rois* in the New Year but group events seem to be occasional affairs. In my experience, the same has been true with sporting groups that I have joined.

FOLLOW THEIR LEAD

So given the obstacles, how have I make any local friends – not counting my fellow expatriates – over the last 20 years? The answer is that I clutch at any opportunity to have a chat with someone new. Then I follow their cue and although it is a very slow process, it seems to be the one that works best. I take the time to talk to people outside the school gate, at the local *vide-greniers* (second-hand sales), at the market and at church.

When the French meet someone with whom they feel they have something in common, you may be invited for tea at five o'clock because that is when the French think that we English drink tea. Alternatively, you may be invited to morning coffee. If all goes well you should invite the person back – and do invite back because if you do not, the French think that you are snubbing them! You may invite them for tea, but for this return visit you could invite the whole family for an *apéritif* in the early evening for drinks and light refreshments – and like that the husbands and children get to know one another, too. If the chemistry is right, a dinner invitation may well follow from your new acquaintances.

It seems to me that, for the French, making a new friend is like making good wine: it takes time and demands a lot of patience, but the satisfaction you get in the end is worth all the waiting. The final product is the feeling of being fully integrated into the community where you have chosen to live.

4
Avoiding the *faux-pas*

As the end of October approaches, so more and more chrysanthemums are to be seen for sale all over France. Large marquees are erected in supermarket car parks to hold the vast range of potted varieties. Chrysanthemum stalls appear at roadsides just like those which a few months earlier had sold melons and fresh summer fruit. These chrysanthemums decorate towns and public gardens right through November, adding colour through the drab, rainy months of autumn.

YOU CAN TELL FROM THE FACE

But, as a newly arrived English woman living in France, it was buying a pot of beautiful, brightly-coloured chrysanthemums which led me to making my first big *faux-pas* – my first big social blunder. I thought that my gift would cheer up a French friend who was in hospital, but as I watched her face drop, I realised that I had somehow made a mistake. What I did not know at the time was that the French traditionally buy chrysanthemums to take to the cemetery to decorate their family tombs and graves! The Catholic Church celebrates *Toussaint* or *All Saints' Day* on November 1st. It is a bank holiday in France and this is when families load their big pots of chrysanthemums into their car boots and place them on their family graves. It is true that perhaps some French women buy chrysanthemums for their gardens or as cut flowers for inside their houses but I have not met many. Either way, I now realise that there is a risk attached to giving this particular flower or plant because of its association with the deceased.

YOUR CHILDREN WILL TELL YOU

It is often my children, in fact, who were born and bred over here, who point out – too often *after* the event – that I have made myself look a fool. I still cannot get the hang of at what point an acquaintance with whom I shake hands becomes someone I should greet with a kiss despite the fact that we use *vous* and not *tu*. Then I forget which people I should greet with one kiss on both cheeks and which people I should greet with one kiss on both cheeks twice over (this is according to where they are from and what they do in that locality).

Very recently – even after living for over 20 years in France – one of my sons told me that I do not get my timing right when I decide to leave a group of people. Apparently I have this tendency to sneak off instead of waiting for the group to disperse.

Tips

- **Do your preparation.** I have made a number of gaffes as a foreigner living abroad and many of them have taken place because I have assumed that I would just fit in. In fact, it takes conscious effort and some preparation to blend in. We were once invited to a very smart work's function and I went dressed –

in what I considered at the time – to be my elegant best. The minute we walked into the room my *faux-pas* hit me: there were probably fifty women present and the number of women present not wearing a black outfit could be counted on one hand. Not only was I not wearing black but I was wearing a red dress: I certainly stood out in the crowd that night. I was inappropriately dressed and the glares from the other women in the room told me so. Thereafter, I made sure that I asked beforehand what the correct dress code would be.

- **Be thorough in your preparation.** Although my son's primary school teacher told her class what to wear for their dancing demonstration for the school fête, it was only after really pressing some of the other mums that I realised that whereas I had intended to throw a colourful bolero together, they were having their children's outfits made professionally!

- **Do not presume that the rules are the same.** When you live abroad, you take your own social codes with you and you need to remember that new friends can find them difficult to deal with. Take our English habit of offering a drink to make visitors feel welcome at any time of the day. It feels so friendly and comforting to us. However, French friends have been quite sharp to me when – I now realise – I have tried to force a cup of tea on them at half past two in the afternoon. For them, it is not necessary and they lose their appetite for the following meal. They had their coffee after lunch and they have tea later in the afternoon.

- **It may be one thing to us but another to the French.** My preconceived ideas about shopping at the local market meant that I pretty well did all the things I really should not have done when I first arrived. I went from stall to stall comparing prices when in fact buying local produce is more to do with eating fresh, seasonal foods with the reassurance that you know personally who has grown or prepared it. French people concerned only with the cost, buy at the supermarket. I now know that I must have seemed very arrogant marching far too quickly from one vendor to another, turning up my nose at the wares at the front of the stand. By observing the locals around me, I learnt that stall-holders keep their very best produce at the side for those satisfied customers who come back week after week: those who spend time asking for tips, talking about the food and on how they intend to cook it.

- **Do not try to change them.** I now know that I should stop glaring at people or creating a fuss, when – in my opinion – they jump the queue. When it happens just for weighing a bag of fruit at the supermarket, who goes next is just not considered important. When taking turns needs to be respected, I have found that the French can do as well as anyone – but the queue just does not look like an orderly line. This has been proven to be the case at parent-teacher evenings when a first-come-first-serve policy usually applies. To an untrained eye, the crowd of parents waiting outside the classroom to see the teacher looks a muddled mass, but they know exactly where they are in their 'queue' even though they have not said a word to each other.

  In my experience too, no matter however many telephone calls you may make to a local tradesman in order to pressurise him to pay a visit, he will only come when he decides to do so. Worse still, the 'I'm the customer' attitude may upset him altogether and you may never see him again!

- **Be sensitive in your reactions.** I have been stunned – to say the least – on a number of occasions by various incidents in the small town where I live. I now deeply regret how my jaw has more or less dropped open in surprise, much to the embarrassment of local people who were simply trying to treat me as one of their own. One of these incidents was when a neighbour had recently died, his wife had him 'laid out' in their bedroom and she asked me if I wanted to pay my last respects to him. I was equally taken aback when my child-minder advised me to de-worm my children when they were young in accordance with the full moon. I realise that the look of shock on my face to these customs would have been very hurtful.

In the same way, I always try to hide my amazement and disbelief when French friends tell me about how they have been treated for some aliment by the touch of the local *guérisseur*.

- **Accept that you will make blunders.** Newly arrived English people that I have met here often tell me how nervous they are when they are invited to dinner by a French family for the first time. I can laugh now at how I must have seemed like a fish out of water at my first dinner parties. To begin with, I was far too early because I did not realise that the French in the area where I live are famously (and proud of being) late. Then, in my enthusiasm to please my new friends, I bought a bouquet of flowers which (I now know) was probably considered to be too ostentatious and which anyway should probably have been sent in advance since my hostess lost a good deal of valuable time trying to find the right size vase. When it was time to sit at the table, I could not contain my disappointment at being told to sit at the other end of the table to my husband – who served as my translator at the time – when in fact the hostess would have spent some time deciding on the placing of her guests beforehand, in the hope of pleasing them. I had totally missed the point: dinner parties are for meeting new people and not for sitting next to your husband!

All in all, knowing what to do and what not to do in a new environment – let alone in a foreign country – does not come easily. But being able to laugh at yourself and shrug off your social blunders does help. To be honest, most French people will accept you for who you are and that is precisely what makes the world such an interesting place. As they say, *il faut de tout pour faire un monde* (it takes all sorts to make a world)!

5
Polite behaviour

When I heard my neighbours talking about the recent *maladie* which was over-running the town, I detected a certain disdain in their voices: they blamed the younger generation of parents for this illness to which they were referring. 'Was it an outbreak of mumps, due to parents not having their children vaccinated?' I asked. '*Non,*' came the answer. 'Was it the recent body piercing mania amongst adolescents?' I continued, thinking that parents were being criticised for not putting their foot down. '*Non,*' they replied. The blight that had hit our small town in the south west of France was *les tags* – which we know as graffiti. The local abhorrence of this scribbling on other people's property is reflected in that as soon as it appears, the local authorities try their best to clean it off.

MUTUAL RESPECT

There is an explanation for this strength of feeling. For people living in small villages and towns in provincial France, respect and consideration for others are principles of behaviour that they wish to live by. *Bonne foi*, which means sincerity and honesty, are codes of conduct for these people, some with vineyards of which proof of ownership – even in these modern days – are not written deeds, but a handshake made a couple of generations ago. When I first arrived here – having previously only lived in large British conurbations – it took some time getting used to an environment where not only do many of the local people know you or know of you, but where there is great mutual courtesy for one another.

PLEASE AND THANK YOU

There are certain words and phrases that are not only signs to the French of how polite or well brought up you are, but that are indicators that you are acknowledging those around you. The rudimentary 'please' and 'thank you' would seem easy enough. However, my children explained to me that – as teachers point out incessantly to their classes at school – it is not enough to simply say *merci*. To really express respect for others, pupils are told to add a name or a polite form of address, as with *Merci Madame* or *Merci Marie-Christine*. Once I knew this, I understood too why mothers at the school gate would halt their child mid-sentence because they had omitted my name.

HELLO

Bonjour is another small everyday word which any newcomer should take heed of. It needs to be said on entering public places – even the *boulangerie*. Shrugging the idea off as a little excessive and being shy about any utterance to strangers, it took a number of cold stares to make me realise that it looked like I was ignoring people. After all, what does it cost to politely say hello to your local fellow citizen?

In order to prove to myself that the provincial French man, woman or child really does address others, I watched and listened while I was sitting in the local doctors' waiting room. I witnessed how when a dozen or so entered in turn, each one gave a general hello to those of us already in the room.

As for shaking hands with people you know, I usually just follow the lead of others: if with their greeting, they stretch out their hand, then I shake it. However, it does seem that those around me shake hands every time they meet.

Even French children at school shake hands when greeting at the beginning of the day and at parting in the evening. In recent years, I have noticed more kissing (on the cheek) between boys with a special bond – those in the same sports teams or class – whereas in the past it would have only been between male family members.

Between adults, a female will kiss or be kissed when she has already met the person once socially. I say 'socially' because a French receptionist at my local tourist office complained to me how newly-arrived English people often insist on kissing her any time they come in for information. 'They obviously think they know me now, but they don't,' she said. In case of doubt, it is better to wait to be kissed first.

VOUS OR TU

When I first arrived, I did not read the signs of polite, respectful behaviour correctly by my misuse of the word for 'you' in French. My French teacher years ago at school explained that there is the choice of two possibilities for the word 'you'. It seemed straightforward at the time: tu is for friends and people you know well and *vous* for those whom you have just met and for acquaintances. I understood that to mean that if I liked someone, I could chose to use the *tu* form and – embarrassed by this as I am now – I must have been seen as very presumptuous and lacking in good breeding. The move from the use of *vous* to *tu* is a mutual decision and people whom you have recently met will ask if you agree to the use of this less formal form of you.

Even the French themselves smile when you ask for an explanation of why they are unable to bring themselves to using *tu* with some people because it is so subtle. *Vous* is a sign of respect for someone and no matter how well you get on with someone, the deference you feel towards the person makes you unable to feel comfortable with using *tu*. So it is that most of my French friends use *vous* to their in-laws! Another example of this is that despite having worked with some colleagues for many years and having got on well with them, we still use *vous* because we want to show our respect for one another.

Interestingly, it seems to me that French women may kiss or be kissed hello or goodbye by someone she has only just met, whereas using *tu* is adopted only after a relationship has matured.

LA CARTE DE VISITE

In my opinion, a very elegant and civilised form of exchange is the French custom of sending and receiving cards. Before coming to France, I had only read about calling cards in Jane Austin novels: how when the mistress of the house was not 'in', the visitor left her card with the servant. Nowadays, a good many French people have their own personalised cards printed – and not just business people. These cards are sent out for a variety of purposes, with differing messages.

There is obviously a set protocol regarding this form of correspondence and it is not always clear for a new arrival exactly how to respond. Last summer, a neighbour sent her card with a message of congratulations to my son on passing an examination. We were very touched, put the card away and did not think any more of it until I was advised that the polite thing to do was to send my neighbour our own card back thanking *her* for her congratulations.

I had a similar experience when I sent a note to a headteacher who was leaving the area, thanking him for his kindness to my children. The following day in my letter box – there it was – his card thanking me for thanking him. My French friends tell me that the rule of thumb is that if you receive a card then you need to respond to it.

The problem is of course, that codes of behaviour are not written down. You can look up a new word in the dictionary but only experience or friendly advice can tell you how to act in the appropriate way. Nevertheless, good manners in small communities in particular, should not be underestimated since even the smallest of gestures and signs of respect can go a long way to helping a foreigner fully integrate into his adopted new home.

6
Give and take

When I first moved to France over 20 years ago, I thought it was natural enough that one of my new acquaintances and neighbours asked me why I had uprooted to live in a new country. When I replied that it was because I had found a job, one of them looked at me knowingly and inquired '*Piston?*' I assumed that she was referring to the name of a firm or an employer and replied '*Non*'. Even when I looked it up in the dictionary, *piston* still left me puzzled. I did not get the gist since the word seemed to be the same as in English: as in a piston of a machine or a pump. I scoured a thicker dictionary and the penny dropped! *Piston* – nowadays more 'correctly' referred to as *des connaissances* – is French for string-pulling: to have friends in the right places. She was asking me if I had got my job because someone in a position of responsibility had used their influence.

My reaction 20-odd years ago was one of surprise that someone who I hardly knew should ask me such a personal question. I also felt belittled that she obviously believed that I was incapable of getting a job on my own merits. But nowadays, I realise that she did not mean it like that at all. Like many other French people, she would have considered being recommended by a friend for a job of her dreams as simply using her advantages to the full; in the same way, I suppose, as some people have good looks on their side and some people naturally perform well at interviews.

RECOMMENDATION FOR A JOB

Universities are the result of *egalité* to the extreme since anyone who has received a high school diploma (such a person is called a *bachelier*) can enrol at a university of their choice. Yet, at the end of their studies, it may well be the one with the most connections who actually gets the job and, in fact, recruiters estimate that many managerial posts are the result of this.

There are those who argue that nowadays when a post as a gardener at the local town hall, for example, is put in the small ads and attracts hundreds of candidates and one of them is recommended by a friend, time is actually saved in the recruitment process – on the condition of course that the person who is being recommended has green fingers.

The same seems to be true in other areas of life. Whether it is looking for a job, getting a promotion, finding a place for your child at the local *crèche* or getting an official stamp on something, you risk being overtaken by someone who is only better than you because they have more influence.

EXCEPTIONS TO THE RULE

As far as school life is concerned, the 35 *académies* of France are cut up into sectors, and towns are parcelled up according to precise demographic and sociologic criteria so that children can find themselves in the catchment area of a school where they know very few pupils. Valid legitimate exemptions to the rules exist: if a brother or sister is already at the school which is not in your zone, or if your child minder already takes her own children to that school. Some parents try and get their children into the school of their choice by using the address of someone known to them who lives close to the school (even their firm's address) and it has been known for a very wary headteacher to insist on seeing a telephone bill, a gas or electricity bill or tax sheet to verify that the family really does live at the address written on the enrolment form.

However, there is another way of getting a child into the school of their choice because each year a commission reviews complaints from disappointed parents and it authorises exemptions called *dérogations*. I heard the word uttered over and over again by mothers at the school gate from the time that my children enrolled at primary school right through to their *lycée*. Some obtain their *dérogation* more easily than others, and if you do happen to know someone with a bit of influence, it does help. According to a report by *l'Education Nationale*, 20% of teachers in secondary education, manage to enrol their children in schools outside their sector.

IMPATIENCE

I have spoken to French people who admit that this culture of using connections is deeply ingrained: that there is something in their *gaulois* spirit that makes them use networking and they go so far as saying that they cannot resist the temptation to cleverly pass before others. As one of my friends said 'whereas the English usually queue one behind the other at a bus stop, the French have a habit of pushing in front'. This admission by a

French person to something that I have noticed brought a smile to my face. There may then be something in the French character that makes them jump a queue.

RED TAPE

The case is sometimes made that it is because life has become so difficult that the French use their connections. Administrative rules are too rigorous, there are fewer jobs around. Places are limited at the *crèche* and in old people's homes. There are only so many council flats and places for your boat at the ports. It is a question of patience: why bother wasting time as your name creeps up the waiting list?

This 'putting in a good word' ethos may also be due to the fact that the French seem to prefer dealing with someone who is already known to their network of friends and acquaintances: it is both reassuring and reliable. On a day-to-day level, they ask amongst themselves for a good plumber (hairdresser, doctor, baby-sitter and so on) before looking in a telephone directory. Then they always tell the plumber the name of the person who recommended him because they feel they will get better service that way. As for the plumber himself, he is able to place his new client in terms of who he knows and can therefore rely on getting his bill paid. All in all, it may be an excellent way of simplifying life.

7
Maintaining your child's mother tongue and culture

Moving to France with children of school age is certainly an opportunity for them to experience a new environment and a different culture. The transition, though, is not always a smooth one due to the fact from the start, there is a new language to master. Toddlers may be able to slip simply into a class of their own age group, but older children may have problems communicating. Whilst language lessons before leaving the UK can only be to the benefit of children, their lack of vocabulary will mean that they may not be able to follow, say, science lessons.

CONTACT THE HEADTEACHER

Contacting the headteacher near to where you intend to live as soon as possible is a good idea because the local education authority (*l'académie*) may provide special needs assistance. There are *academies* that have a support system for children who have just settled in France which is called *Centre académique pour la scolarisation des nouveaux arrivants et des enfants du voyage* or *CASNAU*. Once your child has enrolled at a new school, the headteacher or class teacher may contact this centre for advice and guidance. Teachers are encouraged to speak French at all times and to avoid speaking in the child's mother tongue. Tests of evaluation in all subjects may be given to your child, and time allocated to help with the new language. Generally, a new pupil who does not speak French is integrated into the class as much as possible and even at secondary school they will most probably do subjects like Art, Music and Sport (which require a minimum of French) from the very start.

A child who arrived not speaking any French at the beginning of the year at my son's primary school was well integrated into his new class by June thanks to this scheme. It took much longer, however, for another girl who enrolled at my son's secondary school since, of course, the level of French required in subjects like French and history is much more demanding, and teachers rarely adjust marks for 'special cases'.

REDOUBLEMENT

French children who are not keeping up with the rest of the class sometimes do the year again, it is called *le redoublement*: this is only done with parents' agreement but about ten per cent of French primary school children *redoublent*. It is felt that the children are more confident and at ease. This may well be the case, too, for a child who can hardly put a sentence together, living in a new country. I will come back to this later in the book.

ENGLISH PARENTS AND FRENCH HOMEWORK

English parents are often anxious about whether they are going to be able to help their children with their homework because they themselves do not master their new language.

Tips

- Primary schools are not officially supposed to give written homework and a good deal of what is given is to be learned by heart. You can help your child do this without speaking the language fluently yourself. I followed poems and songs in my children's exercise books as they recited them to me despite the fact that I often did not actually understand what they were saying!

- Some things can be learnt in English. I helped my children memorise their multiplication tables in English.

- In France, schools usually provide a supervised study period (*étude*) after the school day and your child may be prepared to stay if it means getting extra help with tackling homework.

- Teachers in France follow a national curriculum that is more structured than that in the UK, and books that outline the programme are available at supermarkets. Parents are actively encouraged to follow what their children are doing at school so that even if you do not speak French fluently, you will have an idea of what your child is doing at school.

SPEAK ENGLISH AT HOME

There is no doubt that living in a foreign country, gives children the opportunity of speaking a foreign language fluently. However, a child's maternal language must not be neglected: once abroad, continue speaking English at home. (The exception being when there are foreign friends around since it would seem impolite.) Not only is it natural to speak English if the whole family is English, but otherwise your children will talk broken, distorted English – Franglais – which is a shame if you are trying to keep their English as correct as possible. I know families where parents speak English to their children and their children reply in French. In circumstances like this, the children are not encouraged to broaden their vocabulary, nor do their parents have the opportunity to correct their children's pronunciation.

FIND SOME ENGLISH PLAYMATES

It is a good idea to invite other English-speaking children over to encourage your children to play in English. Thanks to other children who had only recently left the UK, my children learnt a lot of vocabulary and expressions that were more fitting to their age group. For this same reason, I encourage them to watch English videos and play computer games in English. It is often in small towns and villages abroad, that English parents need to be the most active to maintain their children's mother tongue.

ENCOURAGE THEM TO READ AND WRITE IN ENGLISH

Then there is the problem of reading and writing in English. A number of teachers have commented to me how surprised they are that English children living abroad often cannot write in English and, when they do, they make basic spelling and grammar mistakes. Sometimes parents do not have the time to help their children. Other parents may feel that they are not capable of teaching their children to read and write. Even when English is a part of the school timetable, it is English as a foreign language and not appropriate to a child whose mother tongue is English.

I started to teach my children to read in English at home when they were five and a half, which was about a year before they started to read in French at *école primaire*. I bought a series of books that are used to teach young children to read at primary schools in the UK. Since my children were able to read a book from cover to cover in English before they could in French, they have always read books in English. This probably explains, too, why they prefer reading books like Harry Potter in English rather than in French.

FIND SOME ENGLISH TIME WITH YOUR TEENAGE CHILDREN

When they were of secondary school age, I set aside about an hour a week to spend on written English with my sons. From time to time this was easier when there was another English family in the locality with children of the same ages and I asked them along for an hour on Wednesday afternoons because school is closed then. I always tried to find something that was interesting and fun for them.

MAINTAINING ENGLISH AT HOME AND DOING WELL AT SCHOOL

When your children are English, it is natural for parents to want them to speak and write English well. It is true, that since our children live in France, we want them to do well at school too. I think both can be achieved.

A HIGH STANDARD OF ENGLISH

There may be a time in the future when you will be pleased that you did not neglect your children's level of English, but rather worked to improve their spoken and written standard over the years. Not only will you be helping your children to achieve a good mark *en anglais* at school, but if you move back to the UK and your children need to integrate back into a mainstream school – or if by choice they want to study there – their level of English will not hold them back.

Even for those not able to benefit from an international school, it is possible – in theory at least – for an English child living abroad to sit GCSE English Language and English Literature in the UK. This requires a great deal of commitment and determination on both the part of the child and the parents. Not all state schools in the UK are prepared to take on an independent pupil because assignments over the two year course need to be set and assessed: finding a willing school takes some research. For the children who already have a French school workload, these assignments mean that extra work has to be completed and sent off to the school in England. Then permission needs to be obtained to release your children from their French school while they sit GCSE exams in the UK.

ADMISSION TO UNIVERSITY

For young people educated outside the UK who wish to apply to a British university but who lack the confidence that their level of (especially written) English is up to it, there are solutions other than having GCSE English. For example, Cambridge Certificate of Proficiency or TOEFL (Test of English as a Foreign Language). Again, families living in France, need to plan ahead in order to find a language centre in the nearest large town which organises these sessions.

The regulations for admission to all degree courses in British universities need to be examined before an application is made through UCAS, the admissions service. Nowadays, all the background research can be done on the Internet either going directly to the website of individual universities or going to the UCAS website (*www.ucas.ac.uk*). Generally, the French *baccalauréat* – which is the high school diploma taken at *lycées* throughout private and state schools in France – is accepted at British universities.

In conclusion, when children move abroad to live, their anxieties often revolve around immediate concerns like the friends that they have left behind and the nagging doubt that they will ever make any new ones. For their parents, the worry of how their children are going to adapt is possibly eased when they move to cities where there are international schools and where other foreign parents are able to share their experiences and knowledge. However, for many more isolated English families abroad, life is a fine – long-term – balancing act; supporting and encouraging their children in an unfamiliar learning environment, as well as maintaining their culture and language of origin outside school.

8
Contact between fellow expatriates

A visitor from the UK recently asked me whether I felt that living in rural France had lost any of its charm now that so many Brits – in his opinion – were buying property over here. He was of the view that from the time Peter Mayle had enticed the British over to France in order to relive his experiences, so many have moved out here that we were – surely – becoming something of a British outpost. 'Aren't you Brits always meeting up and living in one another's pockets?' he asked.

FELLOW CLASSMATES

Whilst most people live abroad to experience the exposure to another culture and a different way of life, it is true that there *are* times when you are drawn to fellow expatriates. Sometimes this is not necessarily a conscious choice. For example, the first English person I met in my small, sleepy French town was someone who had contacted the same French teacher as me. My teacher suggested lessons together since we were both beginners and that it would be more fun and motivating than individual lessons. It was true. We rarely saw each other outside lesson-time since our ages and interests meant that we had little in common, but my French benefited from the whispered English translations from across the desk as well as from our light-hearted rivalry.

I imagine such 'accidental' meetings are more common in larger towns where, for example, English children meet other English children at international schools and then at some point their parents get together. In cities too, where groups of expatriates work for the same firm and come across each other in time, even if it is at the coffee machine. In the countryside where I live in the south west of France though – and particularly outside the holiday season – bumping into a fellow Brit is only an occasional occurrence.

ENGLISH PLAYGROUPS

The extent to which one consciously seeks out fellow nationals, of course, varies from person to person. Nevertheless, even for those of us who have established new lives, made friends with non-English speakers and have become extremely attached to their adopted country, there are times when it is a real pleasure to meet other English speakers. One group that I have felt enriching in this way was an informal children's club that I helped set up. We were a group of English-speaking mothers who decided we wanted to create an opportunity once a week for our children to play in English. Our children had been born abroad, went to the local village schools and without our weekly club, they would have rarely spoken to other children in English. Without the other mothers' encouragement and the routine of organised activities once a week, my children might never have read or written in English let alone known what Bonfire Night or Thanksgiving was all about.

SMALL DOSES

Whilst all of us had the same reason for wanting our children to get together – to speak English – our sensitivity to being called a *clique* made us feel once a week was enough. This balance between a desire to integrate into a new culture and at the same time transmit our own culture to our children was a sensitive one to all of us and particularly to those who were married to Frenchmen.

READING GROUP

Nowadays, I meet a group of English speakers once a month for more selfish motives: access to books. Although the odd English book has been spotted in my local *librairie* or bookshop, the selection is limited to say the least. Even in this day of bookshops on the Internet which enable us to buy easily regardless of distance, some of us need physically to flick through a book before selecting it. (A friend admitted once of her need to smell a book before deciding to dive in for a read!) To call our group an English Book Club is too grand. We are a cross-section of nationalities who meet in an informal manner to swap books and to talk about those that we have enjoyed reading. Interestingly, we are not all English. Some are English speakers from countries like America, Canada and New Zealand. Our monthly exchanges have been an opportunity for me to read literature from other countries and learn about other cultures. Other members – including Dutch, Greek, Austrian and Norwegian – are foreigners abroad who have always read in English.

A noticeable characteristic of these informal groups of expatriates is that although they may start with high ambitions, compromise wins the day. After all, we are people who might never have actually chosen one another as friends under normal circumstances! Some mothers in the children's group wanted more structured activity whilst others simply wanted their children to play. Some of our book group would prefer more of a literary club where we could analyse extracts and this has been rejected as too scholarly. Others would prefer that we are all required to read the *same* book which we could discuss in detail: this has proven to be impractical because some members read much more slowly than others. In any case we have such diverse reading tastes that the choice of which book to read would force someone to read a book that they would rather not read. Another delicate point is whether to limit the size of the group since the bigger it gets, the less likely it is that everyone will be able to discuss a favourite book.

SWAPPING STORIES

More important, though, is how these gatherings have become support groups: a life-line to foreigners striving to learn how their adopted country works. Meeting others in the same situation is an opportunity to exchange experiences and opinions. Cutting through bureaucratic red tape – for example – is more manageable when explained by someone who has overcome it themselves.

Whilst it is true then, that I do meet up occasionally with other Brits, it is not more so now than it was when I first arrived in France. These get-togethers are far from being occasions of reminiscence of something we have 'lost', and we are certainly not trying to create a 'little England' overseas. On the contrary, the tips we pick up from each other enable us to integrate into our new lives more fully.

Education and learning

9
State school or private school?

It is said that about four out of ten French children have spent some part of their school lives at a private school. Some families choose private schools for their children because they simply believe in them. Sometimes the choice is made because parents believe the local private school has a better reputation than the local state one. However, from what I can see in the small town where I live, many parents move their children from state to private or from private to state school depending on the needs of their child rather than on any specific philosophy.

ENROLMENT

As far as state-run schools are concerned, a child must go to their local one in the geographical sector appropriate to where they live. An important point about state French schools is that teachers are allocated to their schools by a centralised system organised by the ministry of education (teachers are not recruited by the headteacher of a school) so it is argued that *all* schools have their share of 'good' and 'bad' teachers.

If you want your child to go to a state school other than your local one, you must apply for a *dérogation* (an exemption) justifying your argument as previously mentioned. Some reasons are taken into consideration – the local school does not offer a particular option, other siblings are already at the school outside your catchment area, the school of your choice is more practical for your child-minder, for example – but your child can only enrol if there is space for them at the school.

As for enrolment at a private school, a family can enrol their children where they want.

LES ÉTABLISSEMENTS PRIVÉS SOUS CONTRAT

However, it is a mistake to imagine that all private schools are independently run, without outside regulation. In fact, the majority of children at *collèges privés* in France go to *les établissements privés sous contrat*. These schools have signed an agreement with the state which pays for the running costs and teachers' salaries. In exchange, the number of taught hours and the teaching programmes are identical to those in state schools. In addition, their teachers have the same training and are inspected in the same way as teachers at state schools.

LES ÉTABLISSEMENTS PRIVÉS HORS CONTRACT

Les collèges privés hors contract are fewer in number and they receive no budget from the state and are therefore paid for by the families that use them. They are completely autonomous in their recruitment of teachers, in the programmes they teach and in their teaching methods. Parents need to be confident of the quality of the teaching before enrolling their children at a private school *hors contrat*.

CHANGING SCHOOLS

If you want to enrol your children at a state school when they have previously been at a private school *sous contrat,* then they will be allocated places at their new state school if there is a place available.

On the other hand, if you want to enrol your children at a state school when they have previously been at a private school *hors contrat* then they will need to sit an exam and you will need to make sure that you do not miss the date, which may be early on in the school year.

If your children are moving from a state school to a private one, you must ask for the transfer of their school records to the new school.

VALUES

The great majority of private schools are Catholic and since state schools are secular – children are not allowed to wear anything other than very discreet signs of their religious beliefs – some parents choose these schools for their religious beliefs. Other parents may welcome the fact that catechism is not compulsory nowadays but nevertheless still choose to send their children to private schools because there remains a strong moral and religious tone. Parents are probably attracted to the values that filter through to their children and to the fact that other parents with the same values as their own send their children to this type of school.

Parents need not be wealthy in France to send their children to a private school *sous contrat* because, after-all, the running costs and salaries are paid for by the state. Parents pay *une contribution*: that is what they can afford, depending on their income.

Some parents say that they prefer the family atmosphere of a private school. The explanation of this is since there is a degree of financial independence, these schools have a tendency to recruit support staff when they are needed, rather than, for example, to renovate a classroom.

RESULTS

At face value it may seem that private schools have better results in the *Baccalauréat* (*bac*) than state schools. However, according to most sociologists who base their findings on official figures from the ministry of education in France, it is the social background of individual children that counts and not whether they go to a private school. The reality seems to be that private schools have better *bac* results because they have more children coming from more 'comfortable' homes and supportive parents.

SIZE

Some parents choose to send their children to private schools in the belief that they will be in smaller classes than at their local state school. Recent studies have shown this not to be the case: in fact the average size of classes at *collèges privés* is around 24.8 pupils whereas at state *collèges* there is an average of about 24 pupils in a class. If this is an important issue, then it should be discussed with the heads of the schools concerned. It is, however, most probably the case that private secondary schools are overall smaller in size than state secondary schools. But even then, in some small towns, there is often an amalgamation of private *collège* and *lycée* (and sometimes primary school too) and consequently the size of the single institution can no longer be considered to be small.

When you move to France with children of school age, you need to be confident that the school you have chosen for them is going to suit their needs – after all, they are going to spend a good deal of their waking lives there. For their part, parents need to feel comfortable with the staff since the system is an unknown one and they – probably with very limited spoken French too – are going to be turning to those at the school for advice and information.

10
The early years

CHILD CARE FOR CHILDREN UNDER SIX YEARS OLD

It is compulsory for your child to have the following vaccinations and when enrolling, you will need to provide certificates to verify these:

- Tuberculosis (BCG).

- Diphtheria-Tetanus-Polio (DTP).

La Crèche

This is a day nursery, usually run by the municipality, parents paying according to their income. The *crèche* cares for young infants from two and a half months to three years for about 11 hours a day, in small groups with qualified staff. Many working mothers therefore opt for this solution to child care. *La crèche* is open from early in the morning to early evening, except for weekends and holidays. Working mothers rest assured that the quality of supervision that their children receive at the local *crèche* stimulates their child's development. As these places are often limited, enrolment needs to be done during early pregnancy!

La Halte-garderie

This is where young infants under the age of six years learn to socialise with other children. It offers care for children whose mothers who do not work, or who work part-time. Children may attend a few days or half-days per week, as the parent chooses. There is usually a small fee to pay. Your local town hall (*mairie*) will give you the details.

For very busy working mothers, the *halte-garderie* is not the most practical solution since they need to find another means of child care on the days when the child is not at the centre.

Une Assistante Maternelle Agréée

Some French mothers prefer to leave their children in a more intimate environment than a collective one and they may choose the approved, registered child minder, called an *assistante maternelle agréée*. The child minder looks after one to three children from two and a half months to three years old, at her home full time. The child develops in a family environment, with other children with whom he or she can play. This tends to be the option for the practical working mother because the *nourrice* (the adult word for child minder) or *nounou* (the child's word) can even look after their child even if he or she has a slight cold or a high temperature, which is not possible in a collective environment.

La Nourrice à Domicile

This is the option for parents who prefer their child to be cared for all day at their own home, and some parents are entitled to tax relief for this service. This formula is ideal for working parents who do not want to interfere with their child's routine. *La Garde Partagée* is when two families employ the same child-minder who looks after their children at one or the other's homes.

PRIMARY EDUCATION: *EDUCATION PRIMAIRE*

Who's Who?

The headteacher is called *le directeur* or *la directrice*.

The teachers are called *l'instituteur* or *l'institutrice,* one class teacher teaching all subjects, usually in the same classroom.

L'École Maternelle

For ages two to six, this provides optional education for children, since school is not compulsory until the age of six. Provided by the state, it is free and although it is, in principle, available from two years old, this is only the case if there is space. If there are fewer places than applicants, then older children will be given preference. I found that preference was also given to children of working mothers – remembering that the *maternelle* is free, whereas the other child-care solutions provided by the municipality are not.

In general, French mothers consider it necessary that their children become used to living in a group with others of the same age. They need to share activities, communal space and learn the rules of collective life. They believe that through contact with adults and other children, their children have the opportunity of developing their language and that school plays an irreplaceable role in children's discovery of the world and culture, through conversation and play.

Very often, mothers prefer their small toddlers to attend for certain mornings, for example, and not all day and every day. Some mothers only send their children to *maternelle* in the mornings for their first years since they only spend much of the afternoons in bed anyway, so that it makes no difference if they sleep at home. This often suits *la directrice*, since otherwise she may not have a place for all the children all day.

How and when to apply

Apply at your *mairie* (local town hall) for your *certificat d'inscription* by June before the September you want your child to start. You will need to show:

- Your *livret de famille*. If you do not have one, you will need to provide essential information including your child's birth certificate
- Proof of up-to-date vaccinations supplied by your doctor
- Proof of your address.

Then, in order to enrol at the school itself, you need to take:

- Your *livret de famille*

- Proof of up-to-date vaccinations supplied by your doctor
- The *certificat d'inscription* issued by the *mairie*
- A certificate of health and school readiness issued by your doctor.

Children who are two at the start of the new school year are accepted if they are sufficiently mature and 'socialised'. In practice, this means if they are potty trained. If the child turns two before the end of the year and the school has a place, the child may be admitted.

The classes at *maternelle* are divided into age groups and are called:

Petite Section: 2–3 years

Moyenne Section: 3–5 years

Grande Section: 5–6 years.

École Élémentaire

For children aged six to 11, this is where the beginning of compulsory education takes place.

How and when to apply

Your child must be enrolled at an *école élémentaire* by the June prior to the September start of school.

If you are new to the area or if your child did not attend the *maternelle*, you must apply to the *mairie* for a *certificat d'inscription* to your assigned school in the area. You need to take:

- Your *livret de famille* or birth certificate
- Proof of up-to-date vaccinations
- Proof of your residence in the commune.

Then you need to enrol at the school itself. You need to take:

- Your *livret de famille* or birth certificate
- Proof of up-to-date vaccinations
- The *certificat d'inscription* issued by the *mairie*
- A certificate of health and school readiness issued by your doctor.

It is not compulsory that your child attends your local, assigned *école élémentaire*, but specific applications must be made through your *mairie* if you do choose a 'non-local' school. You must request a *dérogation* (an official exemption) to apply to a school outside your catchment area. Parents can approach schools directly for enrolment (in addition to the *mairie*) and at some schools it is at the headteacher's discretion whether entrance for a pupil from another catchment area is allowed.

Classes at *écoles élémentaires* are divided into age groups and follow a set national curriculum and programme.

In small villages (and some towns where the population is declining) however, when numbers of pupils are low, different age groups are put together in the same class. Despite this mixture of age groups, though, the teacher will nevertheless teach the appropriate programme to the appropriate group.

57

Cours Préparatoire (known by its abbreviated form *CP*): 6–7 years

Cours Élémentaire 1 (known as *CE1*): 7–8 years

Cours Élémentaire 2 (known as *CE2*): 8–9 years

Cours Moyen 1 (known as *CM1*): 9–10 years

Cours Moyen 2 (known as *CM2*): 10–11 years.

11
Secondary education

COLLÈGE ENSEIGNEMENT SECONDAIRE

Secondary education is compulsory until the age of 16. The first cycle for pupils aged 11–15 years takes place at a *collège*.

As with elementary schools, you should register at your local *mairie* by June or sooner if you want your child to be schooled outside your catchment area.

Otherwise, enrolment forms are distributed to children in the spring term whilst they are in their CM2 classes. Parents are asked to indicate whether their child will be a border, whether their child will be having school meals or be going home for lunch and which modern language they intend to study. This sheet is returned to the CM2 teacher and parents are contacted by their local *collège* who will send further details.

Year groups in secondary schools in France are named in descending order: the youngest pupils being in the 'sixth' year:

• *Sixième*: written as *6ème*: for pupils from 11–12 years

- *Cinqième*: *5ème*: 12–13 years
- *Quatrième*: *4ème*: 13–14 years
- *Troisième*: *3ème*: 14–15 years.

Lycée

This is where those aged 15 to 18 follow a general education. Admission depends on the pupil's school record, usually in the last term of *collège*.

Only the first year is compulsory for pupils at *lycée*: discussions at the end of *seconde* decide future studies.

Over the final two years at *lycée*, pupils specialise in their chosen areas. The final exams are the *Baccalauréat* (the '*bac*').

The year groups are called:

- *Seconde*: for pupils from 15–16 years
- *Première*: 16–17 years
- *Terminale*: 17–18 years.

WHO'S WHO AT *COLLÈGE* AND *LYCÉE*

Le Principal and Le Proviseur

The head of a *collège* is *le principal* and the head of a *lycée* is *le proviseur*. In both cases, the head is responsible for the organisation, management and safety of the establishment as well as the teaching methods.

The head chairs school meetings and has the final say regarding option choices for your child. An appointment needs to be made for a meeting.

L'Adjoint au chef d'établissement

Le principal/Le proviseur often has a deputy, *l'ajoint*. Deputies may be delegated to chair meetings and since they are more available than the head, they may be who you see regarding a problem.

Le Conseiller Principal D'Education

Often known in the abbreviated form, *le CPE*, with the help of a team of *surveillants*, ensures that pupils are punctual and that their school attendance is regular. *Le CPE* notifies parents about any discipline problem that has arisen at school. It is to *le CPE* that you send your child's medical certificates and notes justifying why your child is late.

The role of *le CPE* goes even further since, being a full member of the teaching staff, he or she helps pupils in difficulty face up to their responsibilities, going as far as arranging tutorials if need be. *Le CPE* trains the elected class delegates to take their position seriously and is closely involved in the organisation of school exams, school exchanges and outings.

Les professeurs

Pupils have *un prof* (a teacher) for each subject and the child must adapt to their particular approach. Pupils change rooms for each subject taught.

Those wishing to train as a teacher in France are selected on their academic merit. They are not appointed by headteachers but centrally by the ministry of education. They are effectively civil servants for life.

Team teaching is the exception rather than the rule and general co-operation between members of staff can be lacking amongst this highly individualist profession.

A national curriculum means that all teachers in all subjects follow the same programme of studies.

Le Professeur Principal

The class teacher (or form teacher) is the person to see if a parent has questions regarding option choices and concerns about general progress. *Le professeur principal* takes a lead at the three *conseils de classe* (class meetings for teachers and delegates) a year and coordinates what your child's teachers feel about your child. *Le professeur principal* is the one who writes the general comment at the bottom of your child's report.

WHAT'S WHAT AT *COLLÈGE* AND *LYCÉE*

Réunions parents-professeurs

Parent-teacher evenings take place once a year when you get the chance to meet your child's teachers. However, these can be very chaotic affairs since appointments are usually not made beforehand and parents wait around for their turn to see the teacher. Given that the French do not queue in an orderly manner like the English, it is often not easy to work out where you are in what seems to be a small crowd. Patience is required.

Teachers themselves are the first to point out that parent-teacher evenings are not the place to discuss real problems – you should make an appointment in order to talk at length.

Le carnet de correspondence

Sometimes known as *Le carnet de liaison*, this is a link between family and school and every child has to carry *le carnet* round at all times.

School rules are outlined (and have to be signed by parents and pupil), absence and lateness is justified by the parent and checked by the school. Pupils note down timetable changes, parents' meetings, outings and school results for their parents to acknowledge.

If your child has a difficulty in a particular subject, you can ask for an appointment with the subject teacher concerned. To do this, you need to fill in the appropriate box in your child's *carnet de correspondence*. Your child will then show the subject teacher the box that you have completed in the *carnet* and the teacher will complete the box with the date and time of when he or she can see you. In the past, I have tried to make an appointment over the phone through the school secretary (hoping to speed up the process, since pupils do not necessarily see every teacher every day and teachers are not required to be at school when they do not teach) only to be told that appointments with teachers are not made in that way and that I needed to complete the *carnet*.

Le bulletin trimestriel (the termly school report)

A *conseil de classe* takes place at the end of each term when the class teachers meet. After this meeting, the school reports are sent to parents by post.

Marks and teachers' comments appear for each subject as well as a comment by the headteacher or one of the deputies on the pupil's work and attitude generally.

Le cahier de textes or *agenda*

Each pupil (under the instruction of the subject teacher) notes down homework which has been set in this, with the date by which it has to be completed. Parents can in this way inform themselves of what their child is doing at school and can help organise their work at home.

The class timetable

The day may begin and end at different times every day, depending on how many lessons a child has.

There may be free periods during the day when the pupil has no lessons. During these hours a child may work in the *salle de permanence* which is a supervised study room or the *centre de documentations et d'informations (CDI)* which is the school library.

Parents also have the option of allowing their children to leave the school premises when they do not have lessons or when their teacher is absent: they declare their wishes at the beginning of the school year and this is stated on their child's *carnet de correspondence*. This explains why you see children of school age out of school during the school day, throughout the school year.

In my small town the majority of parents give their permission so that their children can go home when they do not have lessons.

The school timetable is often not the same every week and weeks are called Week A and Week B. This is due to half-classes being taught in science or language labs for example, when smaller groups are necessary for safety or teaching is more effective in smaller groups. Although parents find this confusing, pupils themselves get used to the idea that they have different lessons on alternate weeks.

12
La rentrée and shopping for the French school year

Go into a local supermarket in France over the last fortnight in August and you will feel it in the air. Visit a stationer's and the atmosphere will be positively buzzing. The French even have a word for it: *la rentrée*. It is the run up to and the start of the new school year.

When I first arrived in France and with no children, I could never understand what exactly everyone was buying – after all there is no uniform to buy since very few pupils in France wear one and certainly none in the town where I live.

Nowadays, as a mother of two teenage boys who go to local state schools and having undergone a fair number of *rentrées*, I know exactly what parents up and down the country are buying.

BUYING A SCHOOL BAG

Firstly, there is the school bag. Some research is undertaken before its purchase and I am not talking about brand names either. There are good reasons for buying your child the best school bag you can afford. All children, even those at primary school, have homework so textbooks as well as exercise books are carried home. Secondary school children carry *all* the exercise and textbooks they will need for any one morning or afternoon to and from school – that is if they go home for lunch. Those who stay at school for lunch carry all their exercise books and textbooks for the whole day with them. My children's bags – books, sports kit and all – have weighed about eight kilos at times! There is not the system of personal desks in form rooms and lockers are limited in number in most schools. Teachers (in other than primary schools) do not have extra sets of textbooks in the classrooms and in any case their job is to teach not to provide books.

All this lugging around of heavy satchels and back packs – and up and down three flights of stairs as in the case of my sons – lead French parents to choose their children's bags carefully in order to avoid back-ache at the end of the day. This always comes up as a point of contention at school meetings, but the nearest thing to any sympathy on the part of the teachers is to allow one of two pupils sitting together to bring in and share their textbook. Teachers are usually loathe to make even this compromise because if one of the two children is unexpectedly absent, then the other is without a textbook for the lesson.

Local supermarkets circulate fliers and publicity with these concerns in mind. Not only are the dimensions of a bag provided but also even cross-sections of the materials used to illustrate padding and shock-resistance. I have even seen school bags stamped with 'approved by the medical profession'.

LES FOURNITURES

Next on the list is *les fournitures*. (Which is not to be confused with furniture!) All children are expected to provide their own pens, pencils, exercise books, files, writing paper, drawing paper, paint, paint brushes ... In fact, everything that they will use to write, draw or paint with.

At primary level, the class teacher may provide certain things and this is often paid for by the voluntary contribution which is requested of parents at the beginning of the year. As for secondary school pupils, they go to school armed with all they need.

WRITING SLATES

Teachers provide lists of what their classes require and this proved to be a real *mal à la tête* for me in the early years until I got into the swing of things. When my son was at primary school, I had to buy an *ardoise* for him. The dictionary said it was a roof tile and I wondered what a class of six-year-olds could possibly need with that! A kind French mother explained that it was a writing slate that I had to buy: it saves wasting paper when the children start to write and they need to practise the same letters over and over again. Then I understood: writing slates like the ones you read about in Victorian novels. But even then, I hadn't quite understood because nowadays they are actually small whiteboards (needing special whiteboard felt tips) rather than small blackboards.

WRITING PAPER

Paper is another sore point since my notion of writing paper was not the same as everyone else's very specific type. I was overcome by the very vocabulary: *feuilles simples, copies doubles, petits carreaux, séyès* ... Single sheets are for taking lesson notes whilst double sheets are for tests so that the teacher can add up the marks more quickly.

At first, I – in vain – looked for lined writing paper that I used to write on at school and which does not exist here: in fact French school children write on squared paper. Small squares for maths *(petits carreaux)* and larger squares *(séyès)* for everything else. This is explained by French handwriting. Primary school children are taught joined-up writing from the very beginning and each letter begins at a certain point in the square and ends at another. When they begin a new paragraph, they start two squares in, after the margin and two lines down.

Some teachers are very precise about the dimensions of the exercise books their pupils will require and although I have been furious when I have needed to go to a specialist shop to order, there is usually a good reason for being so exact. Often it is so that the children do not have to trim down maps or graphs or sketches before they glue them into their books. One humanities teacher insisted the children write on pink writing paper for her history lessons, blue for her geography lessons and yellow for her civics lessons!

It is wise to wait for the teacher to distribute a list and to stipulate exactly what pupils are expected to bring, because otherwise you may find that what you have bought in advance will only be wasted.

When my sons first went to secondary school, their teachers spent an hour with them discussing the things they would always need in their pencil cases, stressing the importance of checking their equipment regularly. They were told that good presentation depends on their tools and at every *rentrée,* I buy them a brand new pencil case with new pens and pencils to reinforce this idea.

At secondary school certain booklets for use in the language lab or for music or technology need to be bought by parents on the orders of the subject teacher. Since there is a great belief in mental arithmetic, it is usually only at *collège* that calculators get a mention on school lists, with the type recommended.

TEXTBOOKS

The final three years of secondary education takes place at the *lycée* and it is at this point that *la rentrée* becomes 'big time' because parents need to provide the textbooks for their children as well as the writing equipment. Given that pupils need some twelve textbooks (not counting dictionaries) buying them brand new seems an expensive option to many parents. Second-hand book sales are a possibility but since the school programmes often change from one year to the next, parents cannot be sure of selling the textbooks that their children have finished with the following year because other pupils will not be required to use them. Like me, many parents decide to hire their children's textbooks through a parents' organisation. For the cost of just under 80 euros my son has all his twelve textbooks ready for the start of the school year and he will return them at the end of the year. They are all in good condition – now that is what I call parent power! In the last two years of *lycée,* our local authority actually helps with this cost.

SCHOOL INSURANCE

Although *l'assurance scolaire* or school insurance is not compulsory as such, it is so strongly recommended by schools that parents with children of all ages consider this a must to be sorted out at the beginning of each school year. In any case, school insurance is necessary for a pupil who takes part in a school trip or who is part of a sports association. Parents' groups distribute brochures when term begins and a wide range of accident and damage cover is available.

THE COST

It is amazing to me that the majority of parents provide more or less what is required and the overall cost seems to be going up every year. According to the figures for the *rentrée* of 2006, *la Confédération Syndicale des Familles* puts the average budget for a pupil at primary school at 170 euros and 335 euros for a pupil at secondary school. Teachers I have asked have confirmed the cost, but add that they – as a profession – do their best not to incur too much expense since they are often parents themselves. There are both government and school grants available to help families in financial difficulty. Workers' committees, too, sometimes make a contribution. Often parents buy in quantity, which both reduces the price of individual items and provides a stock that lasts the whole year.

L'Association Famille de France estimates that at the *rentrée* 2006-7 parents with children starting their first year at *collège* spent about 202 euros per pupil on pens, paper, school bags, books and other equipment. Given the cost to their parents, French children probably have every interest in taking good care

71

of their school things – otherwise they have some explaining to do at home! *Vive la rentrée*!

13
The local school: tradition and rigour

I have had a number of telephone calls from the UK over the past few years: friends of friends hesitating about buying property and moving to France. The first wave of arrivals was retired couples worried about finding reliable masons and plumbers, but this happens less frequently nowadays. The questions now tend to come from younger families and the vital query is basically the same: 'What will the local school be like?' The answer is always a difficult one since although the organisation and management of schools in general is the same throughout France, they are not identical – let alone in small villages where schools have to cope with declining numbers of pupils. I can only hope that I have given these families a few useful pointers as to what to expect.

THE LANGUAGE

One thing will be certain, everyone will speak French and the main anxiety for parents moving to France with children of school age is the language barrier. The younger the child, the more easily will they cope with the language. Older children may well benefit from some tuition in the UK before leaving for France. Headteachers may well be able to provide special needs assistance in some cases.

LE REDOUBLEMENT

It is possible nevertheless, that the headteacher will feel that in order to ease your child into their new language, he or she might be better off with a younger age group. From primary school onwards, there are often children in classes who are older than the others. This is explained by the practice – which I have mentioned before – of *le redoublement*: when a pupil does not go up a year with his or her peers but redoes the same year again. It is certainly not seen as a punishment and the pupil is not considered 'a failure' in being held back a year.

Although this is done only by agreement between all concerned, it is surprising how many parents are keen on *redoublement*.

- Doing the same year again allows children to regain confidence since they may strengthen themselves in their weak subjects and therefore feel more able to pursue the career path of their choice.
- It also enables pupils to become more organised in their approach to schoolwork and homework.
- Since the year is not necessarily taught by the same teachers, it allows a child in difficulty to 'start over'.

Le redoublement is not a miracle solution however and there is no assurance that results will be better than those of the previous year. In fact, there may also be some false security in the first term when the pupil's marks improve dramatically and this is because the autumn term is often one of revision. It takes some effort to maintain the same progress in the following terms.

A LONG SCHOOL DAY

The organisation of the school day is not the same as in the UK. In France, a day at primary school may seem longer – and more tiring – for young children, with three hours in the morning and three hours in the afternoon. From 08.30–11.30, then 13.30–16.30. Having your children at home for lunch at first rather than leaving them at the school canteen would provide the opportunity to talk over any problems.

The school day is even longer for secondary school pupils – often from eight in the morning until six in the evening. For those living in villages and having to take the school bus, pick up and drop off times make school days even longer and more tiring – especially in those first months when a whole day in French is quite a feat.

Unlike in times past, most schools are closed on Saturday. Primary schools tend to be closed all day Wednesdays as well, but for working parents, the local *centre de loisirs* staffed by qualified child carers occupy the children with a wide range of activities.

Secondary schools are closed on Wednesday afternoons which gives parents the opportunity to organise activities that are not on the school curriculum (like religious education) or which only play a limited part (like art and crafts, music and sport).

LEARNING TO WRITE

My children had a very rigorous, traditional primary school education and learning to write is an example of this. French children are taught joined-up writing from the outset. On the first day at primary school, teachers begin with the letter 'a', and the children copy it out time and time again on their slates or white boards until every stroke and shape is correct. Day two will be the letter 'b' and so on, until day 26 and the letter 'z'. French children write on squared paper that resembles maths paper: the curves and stems of every letter start and finish at precise points in the square.

MENTAL ARITHMETIC

Rigorous, repetitious but successful rote learning is often a feature of French arithmetic teaching. By the time children are eight, they usually know all the multiplication tables. My son answered ten questions every morning in class to the beat of a metronome. 'Five times eight', tick; 'nine times nine', tick; 'six times nine', tick, and so on; the children writing the answers down on the tick. Initially, I was horrified at the stress he was being put under but he seemed to take it in his stride. As he got better, he actually looked forward to the lessons. By the end of the year, it was 'five times eight plus nine times seven', tick; 'three times six plus nine times nine', tick. Traditional mental arithmetic has always been regarded as important and – apart from being shown how they function – there was never any question of calculators being used at my sons' primary school. Even at secondary school, teachers insist on mental arithmetic whenever it is quicker than with a calculator.

LEARNING BY HEART

Parents are encouraged to play an active role in their children's education. Every child has a *cahier de textes* – a homework book for parents to see and sign. Although there is officially no written homework at primary level, there is a lot of learning by heart – poems, verbs, historical facts, *La Marseillaise*.

At secondary school the amount of detail that my children have had to learn in an evening has seemed endless to me – all the counties and rivers of France, a time-line of all the kings, emperors and leaders of France with their dates, lists of grammar rules, chemical compounds – and all tested on the following day.

A NATIONAL PROGRAMME

As previously stated, France follows a standard and detailed national curriculum. To judge by the number of school textbooks on sale in the supermarkets, coaching seems to be routine. There are books to practise dictation, improve arithmetic and perfect handwriting. Parents do not feel overcome by the vastness of education; rather, they feel part of it. If you move to the other side of France and your child changes school mid-year, the new school will be following exactly the same programme.

RECITATION

My children are used to speaking in public because they have always done a lot of recitation at school. After learning a poem at home, they recite it to the class the next day. They learn a paragraph on the Gauls or the solar system and again recite it to the whole class. I used to shrink at the idea of my son standing at the front on his teacher's platform with the children facing him in rows. Then French mothers explained that they believed recitation improves a child's memory. I certainly now think it can give a child confidence.

DICTATION

Dictation plays an important part of the school week from elementary school onwards. At first children are sent home with a paragraph that they know will be dictated to them the following day. French mothers explained to me how they would prepare their children by studying the spellings and punctuation, writing the paragraph out at home over and over again – in the hope that the next day they would be able to write it out perfectly. Given that every mistake made by the pupil is penalised by half a mark – even forgetting a comma – these *auto-dictées* are dreaded by most. For older children in secondary schools, the pupils do not see the paragraphs that are dictated in lesson beforehand and the texts are often by famous writers like Victor Hugo or Jean de la Fontaine from the last century so that the whole exercise is often expressed in a French style that is no longer a current one!

FOREIGN LANGUAGES

Learning a foreign language – usually English – begins at primary school. The emphasis is on oral work and basic vocabulary – members of the family, parts of the body, days of the week – and includes memorised forms of how to introduce yourself and give your personal details. The aim is not formally to teach a foreign language but to accustom the children to hearing and saying unfamiliar words and sounds. By the time they start their secondary education at eleven, when formal foreign language lessons begin, they are used to participating orally. Generally, all children study two foreign languages at secondary school and have the option of doing ancient languages too.

TESTS – AND OFTEN

French teachers – at all levels – believe in tests. My sons have small tests once a week and more detailed ones – *contrôles* – about every two months. A mother knows by heart what her children's average marks are and where they come in relation to the rest of the class.

QUALITY RATHER THAN JUST EFFORT

In my experience, parents and children from a very early age realise that a teacher's mark reflects the quality of the work; that although a teacher may comment on the effort a child has made, the mark given reflects what the work is really worth. If a piece of work is wrong or illegible, a child's mark will reflect this: there are no marks for 'just trying'. This seems an insensitive approach to learning, but children toughen up to it.

The idea that students either know their stuff or don't is illustrated by the fact that exam performance – not continual assessment – is paramount for anyone wishing to pass the general *baccalauréat*.

ALL SUBJECTS ARE IMPORTANT

This is true too of all subjects, not just 'academic' ones. My son never had a painting pinned up in his classroom for a whole of a school year at primary school because, no matter however hard he tried or however much progress he made personally, his paintings were simply not good enough. The teacher would not pin up a painting with paint dribbling down it and, frankly, that is what he produced! He considered this reasonable enough since there were things he could do that others in the class were less able at doing. There is no 'dumbing down' in sport either: if a child cannot master the techniques required for playing volleyball, for example, the mark will reflect the weakness.

OUT OF 20

Throughout school life, teachers mark out of 20. Two out of 20 may seem very demoralising but that is what a child may get if he or she has not produced what is required. Teachers rarely give 20 out of 20 because they consider it impossible to get everything correct – as one teacher explained to me, '20 out of 20 is for God!'

On a child's term's report, each subject will be out of 20 and you will know what the highest and lowest marks in the class were.

Then, there will be an average mark, made up of all the subject marks and again, you will see what average mark the child who was top of the class achieved and similarly at the bottom of the class.

The overall score in the *baccalauréat*, which is taken at the end of secondary school, is not a letter or percentage but a mark out of 20.

THE SPIRIT OF COMPETITION

An interesting point here for newly-arrived families is that not only does the British education system pride itself upon character building (and so effort is important) but that an individual child's progress is seen in relation to his or her own ability.

In France, a child's position in relation to the class is important: on the school report, the maximum and minimum marks are there for you to judge in relation to your child. Entrance to elite educational institutions in France (and to government posts) is not based on whether candidates passed the entrance exam but whether they achieved one of the top marks in the exam.

14

How a parent can help their child to succeed at school

There has been a lot of talk about girls doing better than boys at school and having two sons makes me mildly anxious about their performance during the school year. Is this the year when my two sons will lose their interest and their marks plummet?

What explains why some children do well and others do not? Surely, having a male role-model to relate to cannot be the only major factor to a boy's success at school, as some argue. And why – if girls do so well – are there always girls who are not top of their class?

It seems to me that – no matter whether you live in the UK or in France – for a girl or boy to succeed at school, he or she needs to have guidance and support: motivation and inspiration are required. The school plays its part in providing this but so must the parents. With this in mind, I strive to do as much as I can to encourage my children to get the best out of their new school year.

A PLACE TO STUDY

I have spent some time finding just the right place for my children to study at home. I have avoided the dining table and kitchen table in preference to a desk away from the hustle and bustle of family life. That is to say not too cut off from the rest of the house because it would be too cold and unfriendly. However, the atmosphere needs to be business-like and serious. One of my sons preferred working on his bedroom floor until I realised that the lighting was not bright enough over his desk. Finally, he *really* settled down to longer periods of study when I bought him a softer more comfortable chair.

NEW SCHOOL YEAR, NEW THINGS

I always buy new equipment like pens and felt tips at the beginning of the school year to help illustrate the idea that it is a new beginning and that everything is possible. Ever since the children started primary school, I have made up an extra pencil case of more 'grown-up' type things like sticky tape, fluid corrector, stapler and good cutting scissors to reinforce the importance of presentation and that first appearances of a piece of work can make a difference.

GET THEM INTO A ROUTINE

Allocating time for schoolwork after the children come home, but before the evening sets in, and getting into a regular routine is important. The children and I agree on homework time during the first few days of term: it is 'timetabled' after a piece of cake and drink or after a certain television programme. Even if they 'haven't got any homework' this time is our fixed moment for putting away the day's books in order to prepare the next day's books. Like that, there is no panicking first thing in the morning!

BE AVAILABLE

This study time must, of course, be a time when a parent is available: it is not that I stand over my sons while they do their homework but that I am there if they need me and I certainly ask them to call me at the end. Finding time after a full day's work is easier said than done, but given all the time I spent preparing their feeds and changing their nappies when they were babies, surely, I tell myself, I can find the time now when they probably need me as much. This is an important time for me to show interest and encouragement and to give advice and direction. I thought the computer would make me redundant, but of course many children in the same class have the same multimedia encyclopaedias whereas a parent can point out ways in which to make a piece of homework more original.

This is a time when I look at details too. Generally speaking, a child will only do as well in a test or in an exam as the notes that they have taken in class allow. Often the notes are too brief or there are spelling mistakes. I encourage my children to borrow someone else's exercise book for an evening and together we look at ways in which we can improve the note-taking.

CATCH WEAK SPOTS EARLY

By checking their exercise books from time to time you can actually act before it is too late. I do not let my children's marks drop too low over a period of time before making an appointment to see the teacher. It is advisable not to allow a troublesome subject to get to that point when a child says 'I'm hopeless' at maths, physics or whatever.

The reason why some pupils struggle is that there are certain subjects (languages and maths for example) which are layers of knowledge built one on top of another over a number of years. This type of knowledge-building could be compared to how one forms a snowball. As you pat snow around the existing ball, it grows, but the snow will not hold together unless you pat firmly. Using this analogy, if a child did not learn the multiplication tables at primary school, he or she will probably have difficulties solving maths problems later. If an irregular verb in French was not learnt by heart last year, it is difficult to construct the sentence correctly this year. If parents catch the weak spot early enough and reinforce what the child learns in class, that point of no return may be avoided altogether. Even extra private lessons can only do so much if a child has not followed in class for months at a time.

A CONSTRUCTIVE ATTITUDE

Here a parent's attitude is important. I never blame the school or the teacher because I am a teacher myself and I can see the benefits of a three-way partnership: the child, the teacher and the parent. When I have an appointment with a teacher, I explain to my children that I am going for *advice* not to sort the teacher out or give them a piece of my mind. I would not want anyone aggressively telling me how to do my job.

PLAYTIME

It is important here to get the balance right with school work: I do not want to stress my child into being too frightened about coming home with a low mark. This is where I think extra-curricular activities have their place. Whilst introducing new skills, they are a useful break from school: exposing the children to something different. There is a risk however that these groups can sometimes be competitive. They can be time consuming too. A ten-year-old still needs imaginative play. Even teenagers need time just relaxing in front of the television and sessions with friends fooling around with their computer games.

I do not consider myself to be the perfect role model to my children: that gives the smug impression that everything I do is the right thing. I am guided mostly by what other parents have told me about their experiences: friends who have the same objectives in mind. We are encouraging our children to fulfil their potential and, hopefully, to have a successful school year.

A local market - *le vendeur de melons*

A local market - *le vendeur de saucisson*

La conduite accompagnée

La kermesse

Lining up for class at the beginning of the school day

Children in class

Une danse de classe à la kermesse

The French art of foraging

Preparation for a local *brocante*

Château Smith Haut Lafitte

Spa de Vinothérapie Caudalie

Cognac Blues Passions

Vineyards

Children at a *brocante*

15
Extra help at school, private lessons and distance learning

HELP FOR ALL AT SCHOOL

Throughout primary and secondary school in France, timetabled hours are set aside for pupils who need extra guidance with their school work.

At certain points, like when they first move to *collège* when it is felt that the whole class needs help adjusting to their new environment and greater homework commitments, these hours are compulsory. During these hours of *d'étude dirigées* the teacher explains what pupils need to bring to lessons in their satchels and how to approach homework in a methodical way, for example.

AVAILABLE HELP AT SCHOOL

At other points in their school lives, pupils attend these hours of *soutien* (remedial support) only if they want to, on a voluntary basis. My sons went to these supplementary French and maths lessons, which were taught by their usual French and maths teachers when they were at *lycée*. Since very few of the class went along, the teachers were able to deal with individual problems, in quieter conditions.

THE PARENT'S ROLE

It seems to me that the general opinion of French parents is that teachers teach their set programmes and it is the responsibility of the class to follow – that is to say that the onus is on *the pupil* to learn. School work is marked out of 20 and school reports that are sent out three times a year, have a mark for each individual subject and a pupil's overall average mark out of 20, too. When a child's marks fall below ten – which is considered to be the average score – on a regular basis, French parents take it upon themselves to do something about it.

English families who have moved to France sometimes express their disappointment that the teachers at their local French school do not see it their responsibility to provide extra time or slow the pace of the lesson in order to include their newly-arrived English pupils. Some English parents have even gone so far as saying that French teachers seem to be insensitive to pupils speaking little French in a system that is unknown to them. Seen in the light of how French parents cope with their own children in difficulty at school, the initiatives lay with the family rather than the school.

WORK BOOKS

It is often with the recommendation of teachers themselves that parents buy exercise books or CDs to reinforce what has been taught in class. The joy of the national curriculum is that what the teacher teaches is available to everyone and lessons are not secrets shared only amongst the teaching profession. Consequently, supermarkets and bookshops have entire shelves of books and software devoted to school programmes according to subject and age group. Publishers like *Nathan*, *Magnard*, *Hachette*, *Bordas*, *Hatier* and *Vuibert* have whole series of *cahiers de vacances, cahiers de révision* and so on devoted to this market.

From the time that my children were in their primary schools right through to *lycée*, I bought each year's programme so that I had an idea of what they were doing at school, so that if they had a difficulty with a particular piece of homework, I could at least try to help them find a solution. These books are usually clearly presented and well illustrated and the chapters are usually in the same chronological order as the lessons are taught at school. Those boring-looking books with pages full of closely typed text however, should be left on the supermarket/bookshop shelves because they are not going to motivate or inspire anyone.

PRIVATE LESSONS

Some children are unable to express what they do not understand and no matter how hard some children try to learn, their marks do not improve. Those parents who prefer others, who they consider to be more qualified and experienced to supervise their children's school work, may ask class teachers if they know anyone who gives *cours particuliers* (private lessons). It is difficult to know precisely how many pupils have lessons at home in order to improve their performance at school, but it seems common enough.

Tips

Whether or not private lessons help a pupil to improve their marks depends on various factors.

- The pupil needs to be in agreement with having extra lessons.

- The lessons need to be presented by the parent in a positive light rather than be considered by the child as a punishment for not achieving good enough marks.

- The teacher needs to be enthusiastic and clear about what they are trying to convey and this is likely to be the case if they have had previous teaching experience.

- Both time and place need to be given consideration. Most pupils in France do not have school on a Wednesday afternoon and this is a popular slot for private lessons. The end of the day is a good solution only if the child is not exhausted after a long day at school, which is often the case at *lycée*.

- The objectives must be clear: to help the pupil work methodically and become autonomous.

POPULAR PRIVATE AGENCIES

In larger towns, a diversity of private establishments is available.

One of the leaders of private lessons at home is *Acadomia* (*www.acadomia.fr*). It is said to have about 20,000 teachers available (most of them students) throughout its 65 agencies, who help about 65,000 pupils. The group is well-advertised and it has ties with *Nathan* which supplies its testing and revision materials.

Cours Legendre (*www.cours-legendre.fr*) was first created by a group of teachers offering different types of remedial assistance: work books, summer correspondence courses, intensive holiday classes, individual lessons, internet assistance and so on. Their teachers, in general, work in schools and this professional status appeals to many parents.

Groupe Complétude (*www.completude.com*) offers intensive courses and small groups as well as lessons at home, taught by high-calibre, professional teachers.

DISTANCE LEARNING

Some parents want their children to make the most of their spare time during the summer months so that correspondence courses are extremely popular during the long holiday.

The leader in lessons by correspondence market seems to be CNED, *le Centre national d'enseignement à distance* (*www.cned.fr*). This is a public establishment, within the national education system and under the supervision of the Minister of Education.

Its offers courses adapted to every level of pupil, for all needs and for every situation. A pupil can complete an entire school year by correspondence, prepare for one particular diploma, or revise, or make up for lost time, whilst at the same time attending full-time school like fellow classmates.

The CNED courses include the correction of homework by trained teachers, many of whom teach in schools as well as working for the CNED. They are at the end of the phone too, if the pupil has questions to ask. Material and support needed to follow these correspondence courses are provided: for example, printed exercise brochures, audio and video cassettes, CDs and Internet links.

For those who are looking to reinforce what they are already studying at school, enrolment with the CNED is straightforward, although special permission from *l'inspecteur d'académie* is needed for those under 16 who want to study with the CNED rather than being enrolled full time at school. The courses come at a price, although grants are available to low-income families.

The CNED also offers courses to those with disabilities or who have serious problems with their school work.

Learning without the direct presence of a teacher is, however, difficult for those who lack motivation. In order for this type of 'extra lesson' to succeed, hours reserved exclusively for study often need to be imposed on a child by the parent. If the homework is to be marked, it first needs to be completed and sent back by post within strict deadlines and this is something that parents may well have to supervise.

I recently read that one *collégien* in five and one *lycéen* in three are having or have had private lessons. *Le Centre d'information et de documentation jeunesse* tells us that about 25% of all school pupils and students have needed *des cours particuliers* at some point in order to overcome difficulties with school work or to prepare for an exam. It is a growing market and seemingly fulfils a demand.

16
Options and career guidance

Despite the fact that guidance on options and career paths is readily available in the form of literature which is distributed at school and in the form of organised meetings, it is seen as the parent's role to seek actively any further information and to make the final decisions for their child.

Teachers in France are extremely respectful of the rights and freedoms of others. In the same way that they do not express views on politics or religion, they will rarely express their opinions on important decisions like options and careers unless a parent asks for it.

THE CHOICE OF LANGUAGES

All children following general education in secondary schools have to choose two foreign languages, irrespective of their grades or abilities.

In the last year of primary school, pupils are asked which modern language they hope to do the following year at *collège* as their first language (*Langue Vivante 1* or *LV1*). They may have already had initiation classes and so have a good idea of what to choose, but they may opt to do another one.

At the end of their *cinquième* when they are 13, they opt for their second language (*Langue Vivante 2* or *LV2*).

The question of whether to do a third language may also be raised when they are 15, just before they move to *lycée*.

The choice of which language is, in practice, a limited one since most schools only actually offer German, English and Spanish. It is said, however, that if a group of parents are insistent enough, they may be able to persuade the school to offer another language.

STRATEGY

About 60% of pupils choose English as their first language and Spanish is the most popular *LV2*. Most parents make the decision based on which language is likely to help them get a job, and English is generally considered indispensable. There are parents, though, who push for their children to do Chinese for example since they think this will be an important factor if their children are to be employable in the commercial world.

Some parents feel that German, with its sentence structure and declension is difficult, and some that Spanish is easy for the French. Others argue that Spanish, being close to French creates confusions and English is difficult to pronounce because of its exceptions to the rule.

I have met parents who have a certain strategy in mind when

they choose their child's languages. A few parents tend to opt for German as the first language since it is considered to be a more difficult language: this choice – they argue – may put their children in a form with brighter pupils since, for the purposes of timetabling, they will be grouped together. *Proviseurs* have been known to foil this attempt to create an elite class by putting the pupils who do German *LV1* in all forms.

DISAPPOINTMENT AFTER ALL THOSE YEARS

Given that French pupils study at least two modern languages for (at least) seven years at school, it is understandable why a good number of them feel disappointed that they do not speak more fluently. I have even heard parents say that the time would have been better spent on mastering their own language! Language teachers will argue that a foreign language is like a sport or a musical instrument that any progress depends on regular practice. They also make the point that parents are being unrealistic in their expectations since even the very best language students at school are far from being bilingual.

CLASSICS

At *collège*, in *5ème* pupils may usually begin Latin when they learn the basics of the language and its history, and in *3ème* they may begin Greek. Since studying these subjects means supplementary hours for the pupil, parents are usually pragmatic about whether their children can manage the extra workload and weigh up the risks of their child's overall marks plummeting. At this point in a child's schooling, it seems that it is generally the most able pupils who choose to do Latin and Greek. However, pupils may have another opportunity to take them up when they go to *lycée* and even the option of a third modern language.

DECISIONS AT THE END OF *COLLÈGE* – WHERE TO NEXT?

From when your children enter *3ème* – the last year at *collège* – you need to read all the brochures and information sheets sent home regarding their future. It may well be the case that they would be better suited to a more professional environment than the general one at *lycée*, in which case you need to investigate the appropriate career path.

From entering the final year in *3ème*, a pupil's marks in all subjects need to be carefully followed by parents. Entry into *seconde générale* requires a good standard in all subjects. After receiving the first term's school report with your child's marks over the first few months of the school year, you may well need to make appointments to see subject teachers and to ask for their advice.

Even if it seems clear that your child is suited to *lycée* and will follow the general programme, there will still be the need to choose from a list of *enseignements de détermination* and, in addition, perhaps an *option facultative*.

During the second term you will receive a sheet – *Les intentions d'orientation* – on which you are required to indicate what your child would like to do after *3ème*. The team teaching your child will express their views in March/April at *le conseil de classe* and their definite decision is made in June at the third *conseil de classe* of the school year and, although parents may appeal, the final decision is made by the headteacher.

DECISIONS AT *LYCÉE* – WHICH *BAC*?

Over the course of the first year at *lycée* – *la seconde* – pupils decide which *bac* (high school diploma) they will take. This depends on both what the pupil wants to do and the results during the year. There is the choice between three general *bacs* and eight technical *bacs*.

Redoubler, in other words to re-do *la seconde,* is a solution that is often chosen by pupils who have been felt to be too weak to go into a class of their chosen *bac*: pupils re-do *la seconde* in order to improve their marks, become more confident and be in a better position to enter the final two years of *lycée* enabling them to better study the *bac* of their choice.

It is during *la seconde* that it may become apparent that a pupil would be more suited to a professional career path (*Le brevet d'études professionnelles* – *le BEP* – or an apprenticeship, for example).

It is during the month of February of a pupil's *seconde* that parents have to complete a form expressing their intentions which form the basis of a dialogue with the members of staff. In May a definite decision has to be made by parents and children, which is then discussed by the teachers who – in June at the final *conseil de classe* – indicate their position on the choice. A parent may make an appeal.

HOW A PARENT CAN HELP

Options and career choice is not the choice of the parent but that of the pupil. However, a parent can play a positive role as an advisor.

Tips

- Take the time to think over the decisions taken. Do not wait until the sheet has to be handed in to talk about preferences.

- Try and be one step ahead: some decisions made early on at *collège* may limit career paths.

- Certain paths are selective and admission is not automatic. Find out the details in advance.

- You can help your children examine their interests. You know them best and you know their strengths and weaknesses.

- Parents can help their children see the difference between an interest as a hobby and an interest as a job.

- You can point out the appropriate career path.

- Parents can help their children see the good and bad aspects of a profession and can help them stand back and look at a career in the cold light of day.

WHO FAMILIES CAN APPROACH FOR HELP

- *Le professeur principal* (the form teacher) follows your child's progress throughout the school year and because of his or her contact with their colleagues, has a global vision of the situation.

- *Le conseiller d'orientation* (careers councillor) who is attached to the school will give more precise answers to questions regarding career paths.

- Make appointments to see individual subject teachers (and not just during a parent-teacher evening when time is short) to ask for their advice and opinions on your child's strengths and weaknesses.

- See the headteacher who holds the central position in the school.

- Quiz other parents and older pupils for their advice and tips on decisions that they have made.

WHERE FAMILIES CAN FIND HELP

- Information on courses and careers can be found in the school library, *Le CDI (Centre de documentations et d'informations)*.

- *Les CIO (Centres d'informations et d'orientation)*. There are at least 600 of these careers information centres in France where you can get details on which courses are taught where, what qualifications you need and so on. Young people can make an appointment with a councillor who will point them in the right direction.

- Schools distribute *ONISEP (Office national d'information sur les enseignements et les professions)* brochures which help families explore the options available to them. For example, *Après la troisième* should be studied attentively by parents before pupils move on to *lycée*. Each year *ONISEP* publishes a thorough catalogue *Après le bac* outlining establishments of further education, diplomas available, information on professions and so on, with contact details. A regional guide to *Après le bac* is also available and distributed at *lycée* during *terminale* (the last year of *lycée*).

- Internet sites like the *ONISEP* site (*www.onisep.fr*).

- School meetings are organised to inform parents and to answer their questions.

- *Des journées portes ouvertes* or open days are organised for parents and pupils who want to visit their new *collége* or *lycée*. For older pupils, this is an opportunity for them to visit their future centre of learning and to meet teachers and students.

- *Les salons d'information sur l'orientation* are sometimes advertised in the press since they usually take place in larger towns. These exhibitions are of particular interest during the last year of *lycée* when the wider picture of available studies and careers paths need to be investigated.

17

Le Baccalauréat

A poll in a French magazine for teenagers announced recently how 84% of those over the age of 16 had confidence in their school system. Despite any scepticism I might have about polls in general, I would agree that there does seem a positive attitude here towards the examination that students take at the end of their school life: that their *baccalauréat* is something worth working towards.

NOT JUST ONE EXAM

The French *baccalauréat* (not to be confused with The International Baccalaureate) is not just one single two-year course with a set exam at the end of it. There is a diversity of *bacs* available.

There are three general *bacs* – literature, economics/social studies and science – each having a specific character, but all aimed at those who hope to continue their higher education after they have left *lycée* (secondary school).

Then there is a choice of technical *bacs* which are a careful balance of general disciplines and technical ones: the aim being to develop a student's general culture and to initiate technologies like electronics and agronomics and even areas like accounting, music and dance and hotel management.

THE RIGHT PROFILE FOR THE RIGHT *BAC*

Students select the *baccalauréat* that is appropriate to their profile. In other words, it is not simply whether a pupil is good at a group of subjects but whether their interests in general (and therefore their future career) have a specific orientation.

- A good literature student likes reading and writing, is keen on languages and has an analytical mind.

- Those who choose the economics/social studies *bac* are curious about the world, about the important social and economic questions, and know how to write and synthesise.

- Those doing the science *bac* will not only be interested in the sciences and experiments but be rigorous in their approach and be comfortable thinking in the abstract.

- The profile for those following the technical *bacs* is that they prefer the concrete; they like communicating and are curious about the environment of the work place.

CORE SUBJECTS

Regardless which *bac* a student chooses, general culture is nurtured and is geared to their particular profile. Maths for an economics/social studies student will focus on percentages, statistics and graphs, for example, allowing them to interpret studies.

There are core disciplines that *all* students study: French, maths, a science, at least one foreign language, history and geography, citizenship, philosophy and sport. Even for those students wishing to follow a more technical career, it is felt that they need a certain level of education across the board. Naturally, French is a must for all, so that all young people are able to write correctly and express themselves eloquently. English is also taken in every *bac*, even the technical ones in order to understand English documents. All students have to study philosophy, the objective being to understand the world, to prepare the students for life and to succeed in it and also to help them to see themselves as citizens.

COEFFICIENTS

On the other hand, the weight or coefficients that each of these subjects carries differ according to the *bac*. For a student taking the science programme, for example, French will count for a smaller part in the over-all mark than maths. Options within the programmes also have varying importance. In this way, a course comes very close to being made-to-measure: students not only get to chose programmes that are relevant to their career path, but within that programme they get to chose which subjects will count more towards their final *bac* grade.

SPECIALISATION

Despite the broad base of the curriculum, specialisation nevertheless plays an important part *en terminale*, the final year. Science students will spend up to three and a half-hours extra a week on their chosen option. For example, a pupil may select maths or chemistry and physics.

TOUGH

There is a rigour that I admire in the French school system. Regardless of the subject, spelling and grammar are considered to be important so that even in a history or biology test, students can be penalised for their poor French.

The same applies to presentation. I remember my son sharpening his coloured pencils and practising his shading, as well as his printing of small words and working out how much information was too much in preparation for drawing his map in his geography exam.

The overall score in the *bac* is not a letter, but a mark – of course – out of 20. This preoccupation with accuracy and no over-rewarding for modest achievement is evident in foreign language teaching where the 'have-a-go' attitude is rare amongst teachers.

Most exams are taken at the end of *terminale* and there is very little, if any, continuous assessment.

SITTING THE WRITTEN EXAM

Pupils sit (*passent*) their written exams in June and they are notified whether they have passed (*ont*) their *bac* in early July. It is worth making the point here that many English speakers mistakenly assume that the verb *passer* means to pass whereas in fact it means to *take* an exam.

PASS MARK

Candidates pass the *bac* if they have an average overall mark of at least ten out of 20. A series of distinctions is given for those with 12 or over. They have failed if they have less than eight out of 20. Those with between eight and ten out of 20 have a second chance: they have an oral examination based on two subjects they have studied and it is here that course work *may* be taken into consideration.

Le Ministère de l'Education Nationale, in its annual report on schools, makes the point that in 2005 France spent nearly twice as much on education as it did in 1980. The consequence of this being that there is a real diversity of studies available to secondary students, and fewer and fewer students are leaving school with no qualifications of any sort. It is true that, as in the UK, there is negative press. For example, we read that despite this huge investment in education, French children are not at the top in comparative studies. Value for money is being questioned. But given how close this subject is to everyone's hearts and how everyone has an opinion about schooling, can you ever satisfy all of the people all of the time?

18
Working towards citizenship in French schools

Listening to a group of school children talking recently, I was surprised to hear an 11-year-old comment on how 'it is the responsibility of every citizen to vote'. Big words from children so young! *Lycéens* too, are frequently seen expressing their views by marching in the streets, confident of their right to do so. These are French children and it is clear that the spirit of democracy is alive and well in secondary schools throughout France.

THE SCHOOL RULES

The school year always begins with class teachers meeting their forms for *L'heure de vie de classe* which is dedicated to school life and news: a time to listen to different points of view and to formulate ideas and opinions. The classes study the school rules – article by article – and then the pupils sign in compliance.

Although the articles themselves may vary from school to school, the general sections of the document will be the same.

School life is dealt with: what time lessons begin and end and how the school canteen is run. A section on absences and late attendance will outline obligations for both the pupil and family: the need for a medical certificate if a child is unable to do sport for any length of time or that pupils must report to a certain teacher if they arrive late.

The exchange of information between parents and the school is covered in the school rules: it is the pupils' responsibility to write down any information a teacher wishes parents to have and to get it signed by their parents – and this includes the school rules. It also means that a teacher knows that parents are aware of set homework and test results.

GOOD BEHAVIOUR

Naturally, there is a section on school security: not only do pupils know how to behave in the case of an accident and where to go in the case of an emergency, but also that the possession of dangerous objects is forbidden. After-school activities are dealt with. A lengthy section covers discipline. Smoking and chewing gum are forbidden in the school and it is here where the disciplinary procedure for bad behaviour is outlined.

COLLECTIVE RESPECT

The school rules may be exactly the same from year to year, but all pupils spend time with their form teachers studying them at the start of every new school year to reinforce the notion of collective respect for regulations. The pupil is seen as an apprentice working towards citizenship.

CLASS REPRESENTATIVES

Two delegates or class representatives are elected during *L'heure de vie de classe* in the first few weeks of term. They are formally elected and the class teacher scrupulously supervises the procedure. The candidates make a speech outlining what role they intend to play and the class casts its votes. These class delegates are not simply class prefects but are given a real opportunity to contribute to the life of the school. They may approach a teacher on behalf of a pupil for academic and social issues.

LE CONSEIL DE CLASSE

More importantly, the class representatives attend the *conseil de classe*. The headteacher or a senior member of staff chairs these class councils, which take place once a term. All the teachers who teach the class and two parent representatives (who are elected by the parents) are present, as well as the two class delegates. After the headteacher has opened the meeting, each teacher comments on the class in general. Then, each individual pupil's progress and behaviour is discussed: comments may be made as to why a pupil is not working to their full potential and the pupil delegates might even contribute reasons to why this is so. This review is done in alphabetical order in fairness to the pupils.

Discretion

The class delegates transmit this information back to the pupils in the same way that the parent delegates report back to the parents. Obviously, discretion is extremely important. What is said during the *conseil de classe* about an individual pupil may only be repeated back to the pupil (or family) in question and in private. In the delegates' summary of the meeting to their class no individual or personal detail must be mentioned. The delegates concentrate on the main points that were discussed and any decisions that were taken. The delegates are neither judge nor censor.

The pupil delegates (as in the case of the parent delegates) may comment at any point during the *conseil de classe*: for instance, on the absence of teachers, homework being too difficult or they may express a desire for more information on option choices. The pupil delegates soon learn that being aggressive is not constructive. Naturally, the teachers are considered to be the ones best qualified to make decisions on education and the headteacher always has the final word on contentious issues. However, each member of the council contributes something and it is an example of how the relationship between teachers, parents and pupils is encouraged.

LE CONSEIL D'ADMINISTRATION

A certain number of class delegates are elected onto the administrative council of the school (*le conseil d'administration*) where important school decisions are made, like the buying of equipment and the drawing up or the amendment of school rules. This meeting takes place three times a year. Each of the pupil representatives has a vote like the other members and their voice carries the same weight as that of a teacher or a parent delegate. Of course, the headteacher casts the decisive vote when necessary.

THE IMPORTANCE OF VOTING

All secondary school children in my town are issued with a *carte électorale*, stamped by the town hall, with the words '*Voter est un droit, c'est aussi un devoir civic*' (Voting is a right and it is also a duty). They are encouraged to stand as and vote for their own town councillors.

CITIZENSHIP LESSONS AT *COLLÈGE*

The teaching of citizenship in French secondary schools is compulsory. At *collège*, *Education Civique* is usually taught by the history and geography teacher. The principal objectives are to instruct children on their civil responsibilities and to teach them respect for rules and for other people around them. The election of the class delegate is a concrete exercise in civic duty, as is the study of the school rules.

Important texts on human rights, like the Universal Declaration of Human Rights, the Constitution of the Fifth Republic and certain aspects of the French Penal Code are analysed as part of a general reflection on man's rights and obligations.

The justice system in France and those of other European institutions are discussed in a reflection on the principle of equality. One of my sons studied Stephen Lawrence's death and the consequences of the case during his *Education Civique* lessons.

The importance of public opinion and the role of the press are analysed. Associations and unions are used as examples of community spirit and solidarity amongst mankind.

The necessity for all of us to respect our environment and

heritage are some of the other issues examined. The teaching of citizenship often takes a very practical form, like for example the reading and understanding of an individual's electoral card or the filling out of an Accident Statement after a road accident.

CITIZENSHIP LESSONS AT *LYCÉE*

At *lycée*, the hours at school spent on citizenship are called by a different name and take on a different form. *ECJS* stands for *education civique juridique sociale* and covers areas of education, civics, law and social issues. The history and geography teacher teaches these hours and the objective is to enable the pupils to express themselves on any given topic. They should be able to contribute to an argument, have an opinion, be able to express it and hold their own during a debate. In practice, pupils are often sent to the school library to find information (primary sources like government white papers and newspaper editorials) and to compile a project made up of different sources, which may be marked by the teacher either with a grade or a comment. The idea is to find a problem on which the class can debate: for example, 'Violence at School'. The pupils are divided into groups and must argue for or against, despite their own personal point of view. One pupil takes on the role of *président* and chairs the debate, pupil-secretaries take notes, whilst others observe and have to complete a ballot as to how they feel about the issue at the end of the debate. *ECJS* means that the whole of the class – like the whole of society – contributes and has a responsibility to be concerned by issues that affect us all.

All the new Euro coins in France – like the *franc* and *centime* coins before them – carry the words *'Liberté, égalite, fraternité'* and these same principles permeate – in theory at least – life in French secondary schools.

111

19
Parents' associations

When your child is at primary school, whether it is at *école maternelle* or *école elementaire*, there are occasions when your child's teacher approaches you to ask for a helping hand. The annual school fête – *la kermesse* – may be one such opportunity for you to look after a stand, make costumes and so on. The same is true if the class needs another adult to supervise the weekly visit to the local library.

As my children have grown, however, so I have noticed that secondary school teachers at French state schools only rarely ask for this type of informal help from parents. At *collège*, the only time was when my son was involved in an exchange with a German school and whilst the Germans were with us, I was asked along with all the other parents, to have a drink with them in order to make them feel welcome. Even that scrapes the barrel somewhat as an example of a parent volunteer!

ENCOURAGED BY THE SCHOOL

At the beginning of every school year from *collège* and throughout *lycée,* however, all parents receive pamphlets urging them to join a parents' association, *les associations de parents d'élève (APE)*. Although by no means compulsory, schools encourage parents to join an association since this is the way in which parents work with the staff to the benefit of the pupils.

A parent needs to find out about the federations that are represented at their child's school and although their headquarters are not allowed within the school itself, there will be a letter box or a plaque with address details.

PARENTS' ASSOCIATIONS PROVIDE INFORMATION TO PARENTS:

- If you join one, you will be informed of a variety of aspects of school life and the different measures adopted by *le conseil d'administration* (the school council or school board).

- As a member of the association, you will also receive advice on dealing with red tape on issues regarding education.

- They also inform parents of adjustments to the new school year and changes in school programmes. Special meetings are arranged with the purpose of informing parents of particular matters.

PARENTS' ASSOCIATIONS TRANSMIT INFORMATION TO THE SCHOOL

The channelling of information works in both ways so that the *APE* communicates any problems the parents believe their children are encountering to the school management.

The associations defend the rights of parents and their children. They listen to individual concerns and express this to the school management in the interests of the general good. This is particularly important in France where teachers are civil servants and are not 'hired or fired' by the headteacher. Thus the efficiency of any individual teacher is dependent on their 'professional conscience'.

TEXTBOOKS

Many parents become members of parents' associations because these groups run textbook schemes. Sometimes, parents' associations organise book sales when former pupils can sell off their books to newcomers. Alternatively, a parents' association may run a system of loaning books for the year at a fixed minimum cost. These non-profit sales are to the benefit of parents who do not want to waste time ordering books and do not want to waste money buying brand-new books that their children will only need for a year. What is more, those textbooks that are no longer on the teachers' lists for study are collected up by the parents' associations and given to charities for distribution to schools in need in poorer countries.

PARENT REPRESENTATIVES

You can also represent your association – and represent other parents – by standing for election.

Every association puts forward a list of candidates for elections that are organised before the end of the seventh week of each school year. Parents receive the details on how to cast their vote and this may be done by post. Parents are notified of the successful list.

These representatives attend the *conseil d'administration* (*CA*). This is the decision-making body. It is chaired by the head of the establishment and it meets at least three times a year. The board is made up of members of staff and local representatives, as well as five parent representatives and five pupil representatives. As mentioned elsewhere, this council decides on school projects, the budget and school rules. It discusses matters regarding information to parents, health and hygiene, security and other important issues. It gives advice on ways of widening course options offered by the school. It advises on the choice of school textbooks and on matters relating to teaching methods.

A smaller number of parent representatives voted by parents in the election attend the disciplinary body of the school. This *conseil de discipline* pronounces sanctions imposed on pupils who have seriously breached the school rules, including temporary and permanent exclusion from school.

CLASS DELEGATE

In addition, all classes in the school are represented by two parents and two parent reserves and the associations supervise the allocation of which parents represent which classes. The associations do this by holding meetings when parents may volunteer. You do not necessarily represent your own child's class since there are sometimes too many parent volunteers for one class, but then there may be none for another class: the important principal is that the parent delegate is not representing their own family but a whole class's interests. Once the *APE*

115

have allocated parents and their substitutes to classes, these delegates make the commitment of being available to attend *le conseil de classe* at the end of each term.

THE ROLE OF PARENT DELEGATES

- They should be available to all the concerns of parents throughout the year.

- They should be diplomatic and constructive in their expression of these concerns when they relay them to the teaching staff or to the headteacher.

- They should circulate a questionnaire in advance of the termly *conseil de classe* in order to represent all parents effectively. Class delegates are responsible for relaying the comments or suggestions of other parents of pupils in the class that they represent.

- The class delegate is also required to take minutes of the meeting which are then communicated to the other parents. The general atmosphere of the class, each individual subject teacher's general comments, points that the parent delegate and the pupil delegates have raised in the meeting are included in the minutes that are sent to parents after each *conseil de classe*.

- In order that the report serves its purpose as a link between school and parents, it needs to be written clearly and concisely, it needs to have the agreement of the school and it needs to be sent to the parents promptly. It is usually distributed in class and taken home by the pupils.

Delegates are urged not to include certain personal information in the recorded minutes, however. The teaching staff depend on the discretion of the parent delegate since certain elements discussed are only to be passed on to the family concerned.

At the beginning of their school lives, your child's teacher may occasionally need a parent volunteer for help. As your child goes through their secondary education, schools still rely on parents offering their time and support through their parents' associations so that together they may create a good working environment for the pupils.

20
Food for thought in French schools

Carottes râpées au jus d'orange
Sauté d'agneau hongrois
Haricots blancs
Fromage frais
Pomme

Le choix du chef at the local three-star restaurant? *Pas du tout!* It is a school meal – typical of the fare that my children have eaten at their local schools over the years in the small town where we live in the south-west of France.

One thing is certain, had they come home for their midday meal, I would not have been able to rustle up anything resembling what they are used to eating at school. Certainly not day in, day out. That is precisely the point that is made in the brochure *Votre enfant mange à la cantine* (Your child has school meals). This information booklet was produced on the initiative of the European Union with the support of a number of groups including parents' associations who distributed it throughout schools in France. For my children, never a truer word was written when it argues that the midday meal at school is an excellent way for children to discover new tastes, spices and smells.

A CULTURAL EXPERIENCE

The midday meal at school has been part of the whole cultural experience for my children living here in France. From nursery school onwards, they were served their meal course by course at the table and were encouraged to eat slowly in order to digest their food properly. They have always eaten with a napkin and have only drunk water so as to really savour the taste of their meal. Since even the young children at each table were left to toss their own bowl of green salad, my sons learnt how to do this, as well as adopting the French habit of eating the cheese before the dessert instead of after it. Thanks to dishes that they have enjoyed at school, I have cooked things that I would never have dreamed of cooking before – rabbit, wild boar, lamb's heart, and asparagus. And as for artichoke, they not only encouraged me to cook them, but also showed me how to dip the leaves in its dressing and suck the flesh off! They have learnt that many foods have their seasons and traditions. Above all, they appreciate how meal time is a social occasion for the French – an opportunity for talking about what they are eating at the very least!

A POINT OF DISCUSSION

Given the importance of food and eating to the French, it comes as no surprise to me that most of the parents' meetings I have ever attended at my children's schools – from their first *maternelle* right through to their *lycée* – have spent time poring over this one subject. I have sat through lengthy discussions about what exactly the children will be eating in preparation for school trips abroad. It invariably always comes up in some form or another, no matter what the actual theme of the meeting itself. I remember going to a meeting once about option choices when parents voiced their concern that children were having too little time at the table before they were being hurried away for the next sitting to be prepared.

My son who is at *lycée*, came home recently with an invitation for the family to attend a debate at school which was organised by one of the parents' associations. The subject under discussion that evening was '*La (mal) bouffe de nos ados*' (Our teenagers and junk food). There is a real desire to maintain healthy eating.

QUERIES

Questions and complaints are dealt with by members of staff as a matter of course because it is considered a must that parents should be able to know what food and in what conditions their children eat. Parents may approach either their local town hall or the head of school about the meal itself or the preparation of it. School meals are pinned up on notice-boards in schools for everyone to consult. The meals are dated so that you know exactly when they are going to be eaten. They are written course by course: very much like you would expect on the menu at a local restaurant.

WELL-BALANCED

The school meal is not put together without thought: directives have to be followed. The midday meal has to be made up of a main course based on meat, fish or eggs with raw or cooked vegetables and dairy products and fruit in order to provide the necessary proteins, iron and calcium. Whilst fat content is deemed necessary, it is limited.

The French are as concerned by growing obesity amongst young people as anyone else and that probably explains why my sons have very rarely been served French fries at school. At birth, parents are issued a *carnet de santé* for their babies and they take it along to every medical check-up. Doctors write their notes on the child's development in this booklet as well as plotting weight and height on the graph pages – and they do not hesitate to point out when a child's weight is veering towards the overweight zone on the graph in relation to height. In their teens, with fewer medical check-ups, children are encouraged by the school nurse to regularly plot their own details on these *courbes de croissance* pages.

CHOICE

Those responsible for school meals have a duty not only to provide well-balanced meals, but also to provide diversity. Many secondary schools have self-service and whilst the pupils *have* to have the main course, some schools allow a choice for the other courses. Most school canteens today prepare a substitute dish for children not wishing to eat pork for religious reasons.

NO TO PACKED LUNCHES

Bringing your own picnic to school is only an option if a child has a special diet for medical reasons and the school cannot provide an adapted meal. Even then, parents have formally to obtain permission beforehand and they need to abide by the strict hygiene and safety laws, in case of illness or accident.

SAFETY

Over recent years, French parents have expressed the same concern over the safety of eating certain meat and genetically modified foodstuffs as other anxious parents elsewhere. Parents now have the right to consult a wide range of information about what their children eat: the origin of products, the date limit of consumption, the list of ingredients, the presence of additives or GM food and so on. Just as important, the level of hygiene in school kitchens is verified regularly under the direction of the *ministère de l'agriculture*.

THE COST

The price of a school meal is capped by law and the price paid by families may not be more than the cost of producing it. Families having a number of children are entitled to a reduced price, and families in financial difficulties pay a modified price.

COMFORTABLE

Another thing that is also regulated is ' the comfort factor' whilst the children are eating: the hall itself should be an appropriate one (and not too noisy), the furniture should be suitable and the children should be allowed a minimum of half an hour in which to eat – not counting the time waiting to be served!

About six million children eat school meals in France. The organisation may vary: primary schools usually have a centralised kitchen that prepares the meals, whilst secondary schools generally have their own kitchens. The measures that have been introduced over the last few years concern everyone. They reinforce the safety of food, new nutritional recommendations and the awakening of children's tastes. Above all, there has been an improved transparency of information so that parents may say *bon appétit* with confidence.

21
Les Grandes Écoles

A mother in the small town where I live here in France, recently commented in passing, 'My son goes to school in Paris'. I had the vision of a young boy at boarding school. The extremely proud way in which she had spoken to me and the look of satisfaction on her face made me realise that I had not quite grasped what she had meant. Then she threw in the vital piece of information to clarify the point so that even a foreigner like me might understand – her son was 22 years old. Finally the penny dropped. He was at one of the prestigious *Grandes Écoles*.

EDUCATING THE ELITE

The higher education system in France is made up of both universities and *Grandes Écoles*. It is the *Grandes Écoles* that prepare the administrative, scientific and business executives – or *cadres* – for their place as leaders in government or in private enterprise. Nowadays, over 60% of the chief executives in France's 100 largest firms are graduates of the *Grandes Écoles*.

There is a nationwide awareness that they – rather than universities – are where France's technical and managerial elite are educated.

SPECIALISATION

In the Middle Ages, the higher education system revolved around the University but, from the Renaissance onwards, the royal power felt a need to create more specialised institutions. This trend continued particularly in the 18th century which was a period of industrial development and new techniques. At first military institutions of learning and those of civil engineers, were created.

So it was that the *École des Ponts et Chaussées* (the school of bridges and highways) was founded in 1747, the *École du Génie Militaire* (the army corps school of engineers) in 1748 and the Royal Shipbuilding School, the *École des Constructeurs de Vaisseaux* was founded in 1765. The Revolution led to the *Conservatoire National des Arts et Métiers* and the *École Polytechnique* in 1794. Other specialist institutions of this sort, providing engineering training, were founded during the 19th century in Paris and in other parts of France.

It was later, at the end of the 19th century and at the beginning of the 20th century, that the first *Grandes Écoles* of management appeared.

One feature of all *Grandes Écoles* then is that these public and private schools provide a very specialised course of study.

HIGHLY SELECTIVE

Another common feature is that they have a highly selective admissions procedure. Some require an excellent school record and a *baccalauréat* (secondary school diploma) with distinction.

PREPARING FOR ENTRANCE

Many others, however, require success at an entrance examination that is prepared over one or two years in the special *classe préparatoire aux grandes écoles*. These *CPGE* teach specific programmes which prepare students who have already obtained their *baccalauréat* and who want to enter a *Grande École*.

Given the selective nature of the admissions procedure there are, therefore, only a limited number of pupils who enrol at *CPGE* and they represent about 5% of the total number of those who enrol in higher education – 20 times fewer than those who enrol for places at university. Although very prestigious, many accuse this system of being elitist and contributing to the inequalities in society, especially since the State spends more on these students per head than on those students at university.

HARD WORK

The rhythm of work and the stress at *prépa* are notorious. Those studying the scientific courses are known as *taupins* – moles – because they are so taken up with their studies that they see very little light of day! The aim is to succeed in the entrance examination set by the *Grande École* or group of *Écoles*. But even if students do not get a place, the high level of education that they get at *CPGE* and the methods of study acquired are said to hold the student in good stead for further studies at university or elsewhere.

GRANDE ÉCOLE MAY BE SMALL

As for the *Grandes Écoles* themselves, whilst some of them are only small-scale institutions and are only as big as a university department, others including groups of schools, like the *Instituts Nationaux Polytechniques* for example, have over a thousand students and are comparable in size to a university.

LONG STUDIES

Studies are characteristically long – sometimes up to six years – after the *baccalauréat*. The link between industry and business and the *Grandes Écoles* is reflected by the emphasis on work experience and on specialisation, notable in most programmes.

TEACHERS AND VISITING LECTURERS

The teaching staff is usually diverse because in addition to permanent staff, visiting lecturers include guests from industry. Teaching itself is based on lectures and takes place in small groups working on individual or team projects.

MORE AWARE

There is increasingly a strong emphasis nowadays at the *Grandes Écoles* on foreign language study and the awareness of other cultures. Even the engineering schools are waking up to the fact that they are competing in an increasingly global environment. At least two foreign languages are usually required and taught. Studies and internships abroad feature more and more in the programmes. Often a year abroad is integrated into the curriculum. Over the years European and international networks have been established and have led to cooperation in scientific and technical research between French *Grandes Écoles* and their foreign partners.

QUALIFICATIONS

Once students have completed their studies, specialist qualifications are awarded. For example in engineering, the *diplôme d'ingénieur* (likened to the Master of Engineering or Master of Science), is accredited by the *Commission des Titres d'Ingénieurs*. In management and business studies, the *diplôme de Grande École* is accredited by the Ministry of Higher Education.

BETTER PROSPECTS

Most *Grandes Écoles* belong to the *Conférence des Grandes Écoles,* which is an association dedicated to cooperation between members. Amongst other things, it promotes international partnerships, advises the government on programmes at the *classes préparatoires* and recognises post-graduate courses. According to the *CGE*, 76% of those who had obtained their diplomas at *Grandes Écoles* in 2004 had signed a contract of employment within two months of graduating. This group of newly qualified students seems to have been less touched by the slow economic growth than students leaving other further education institutions. In addition, students graduating from *Grandes Écoles* often seem to be offered good conditions of work in their contracts: for example many are recruited at the outset with the status of *cadre* and many of them hold long-term, as opposed to short-term, contracts.

So it is that statistics seem to show how French employers – many having come through the same institutions themselves – value the particular profile of newly qualified graduates fresh out of *Grande École*. All in all, those carrying such a diploma appear to begin their working lives with a certain advantage. No wonder the mother I met was so proud of her son!

22
Learning to drive: a rite of passage

It feels like my teenage son has been driving me around in my car for years now – and he has! Since he turned sixteen to be precise. *L'apprentissage anticipé de la conduite* (AAC), commonly known as *conduite accompagnée*, allows young people to spend most of their learning kilometres with an accompanying adult rather than a driving instructor. This option, introduced in 1990, offers a real alternative to parents with teenagers wishing to learn to drive. Judging by the number of other cars like ours displaying the compulsory sticker on their rear windows and bumpers, it is a choice many families in France are turning to.

THE BENEFITS

Far from seeing any potential loss of revenue for itself, it was our local driving school that actually pointed out the benefits of this supervised driving scheme to us.

- To begin with, AAC is **less costly** for parents than the classic method where a driving instructor takes out pupils regularly until they eventually pass their test.

- But, the driving school went on to explain, that is not the only reason for choosing the AAC route. The driving school positively encouraged us to supervise our son by pointing out that those doing the *conduite accompagnée* were **increasing their chances of actually passing their driving test.** National statistics confirm this fact: candidates are thought to have an 80% chance of passing the test first time as opposed to 50% for those who have followed the classic method.

- **Insurance companies offer reduced tariffs** to these young people who have done the *conduite accompagnée* once they have passed their tests.

Although the *conduite accompagnée* is accessible to young people over the age of sixteen, any adult can also chose this type of course. Those younger than eighteen must have their parents' agreement.

THE RUN-UP

Before actually sitting behind the wheel itself, the student must complete an initial practical course of about 20 hours at a driving school and also pass the theory test on the Highway Code. Once the driving school has completed the paperwork in which the supervising adult or adults are formally mentioned, the driving itself can begin.

THE SUPERVISING ADULT

The law stipulates that the supervising adult:

- has to be **older than 28**;

- has to have had a **clean driving licence** for longer than three years;

- must also **carry a driving licence** whilst sitting in the car when the young driver is at the wheel;

- observe **drink drive laws**;

- must take the role seriously and **correct the pupil** when necessary;

- ensure that **the driving situations are diversified**: the pupil should not do all town driving or just quiet country lanes.

The pupil should have the opportunity to drive regularly. In addition, a learner driver should not do all the driving on a long trip, but take it in turns.

In most cases, of course, the adult is one or both of the pupil's parents and the car being driven is the family car. An extension is usually added to the car insurance at no cost.

COMPULSORY SESSIONS FOR PARENT AND TEENAGER

The learner must drive at least 3,000 kilometres during a minimum of one year and maximum of three years. In order to evaluate the pupil's progress (and to check that bad habits have not been picked up from the supervising adult) the pupil and supervising adult must attend two theory and practice sessions at the driving school.

At these sessions, driving instructors clarify the point that the role of the adult is not to teach, since the pupil is applying in practice what has already been taught by the instructor during the initial driving lessons. The pupil is getting used to driving in everyday traffic: experiencing both the pleasures and the risks of driving. The supervising adult is an advisor rather than a teacher: a driver sharing experiences.

RESTRICTIONS

Whilst behind the wheel the learner driver is bound by certain speed restrictions: 80kph instead of 90 on ordinary roads, 100kph instead of 110 on dual carriageways and 110kph instead of 130 on the motorway. The pupil may not drive outside France and must always carry the relevant documents.

STRESSFUL

To say that these past 3,000 kilometres have passed without one or two 'tense' moments would be untruthful. When I swap notes with other parents, they feel the same way. The very idea of this kid who was – only five minutes ago so it seems – playing with his building bricks, being trusted to drive your precious car and having both your lives in his hands, is a difficult concept to say the very least. It comes as quite a blow to your ego too – and the driving instructor does warn you – to have to admit to criticism of your own driving!

SAFER DRIVERS

The main argument that convinces parents like me to undergo being driven around by their teenage offspring, however, is that statistics show that with this experience of learning to drive, the risks of accidents are considerably reduced. Our driving school's brochure says four times fewer accidents are had by those having completed ACC than other drivers of the same age. Insurance companies are particularly sensitive to these statistics and that explains why they offer reduced tariffs to young people who have done the *conduite accompagnée*.

FEWER DEATHS

In the area of France where I live the number of 18- to 24-year-olds killed on the local roads are four times fewer than before the year 2000 and the number of deaths of young people on the roads in my county has been cut by half.

DRIVING ON PROBATION

Despite this, the mood is far from complacent. New measures have been introduced by the government to reduce accidents amongst newly-qualified drivers. Driving instructors and learner drivers have welcomed the idea that learner drivers should drive on probation for three years in order to obtain a total 12 points on their driving licence. Over these three years the newly qualified driver will only have six points instead of 12 and must therefore drive with utmost care because the least error could cost them their driving licence. In the UK, drivers are given points for traffic offences; in France the points are removed from the total available (12, or 6 for inexperienced drivers) and on reaching 0 points, the driver is disqualified for a period of time.

For those having done the *conduite accompagnée*, this

probationary period is two years, after which their initial six points increase to twelve if no offence has been committed.

You may be one of the millions of visitors touring France this summer and happen to drive behind a sticker showing the outline of two heads: one small face wearing a smile at a steering wheel and one larger face sitting alongside. When you read the words *conduite accompagnée*, the teenager in front of you is not only clocking up kilometres in order to pass their test when they turn eighteen but is doing so as part of a national effort for safer roads.

The appeal of the French lifestyle to young and old alike

23
The French art of foraging

I was taken aback recently when, on a Sunday afternoon's walk in the countryside, my beautifully manicured French friend bent down and pulled up a bunch of dandelion leaves by their roots and carefully packed them into her leather back-pack. She explained at great length how she would wash the leaves and make a meal of them with fried bacon, a lightly boiled egg and a drizzle of olive oil. I was lost for words: she was talking here about what were – for me – some dirty old weeds she had found at the side of the road! Even the French word for it – *pissenlit* – meaning to wet the bed, is not exactly elegant. But, judging by the numbers of other passers-by clutching their finds, I realised that dandelion leaves were another of those seasonal collectibles that the French love to seek out. The leaves are best eaten before the yellow flower appears; the white stalk towards the bottom of the stem near the roots being almost nutty in flavour. The French, though, eat *pissenlit* not simply for its taste but because they believe it to be a good purifier of the blood. The same goes for *mâche* or lamb's lettuce.

MUSHROOM COLLECTING

Being born and bred in an industrial British city, the sight of the provincial Frenchman or woman bending down in the middle of a field, in order to stash a find in their plastic carrier bags never fails to arouse my curiosity. In the autumn – and very early in the morning – it will be mushrooms and more particularly the larger *cèpes*. People I know tell me of their own 'secret place' where they go back to from one year to the next; so 'secret' that they would never divulge the spot to anyone else, no matter what!

I ask my French friends how they dare eat a mushroom that they have found growing wild in a wood: think of the dangers of eating a deadly poisonous one! They inform me that to check whether a mushroom is of the edible variety, you can go to the *pharmacien* – the local chemist – who is obliged to advise the public on which mushrooms are safe to eat.

SNAILS

Snails are another example of a food that the French are known to collect because they are healthy – being rich in protein – and delicious to eat. Every time I have my water meter read, the official peers under the slab in my garden and asks me if I mind him taking the numerous snails there – and can he have a plastic bag please! I know too that if I see a torch-light in my garden at the end of a wet spring day, it is only my neighbour collecting snails! For days after, he gives me a detailed culinary bulletin of his preparation before eating them. How he feeds them on flour for a time in order to clean out the their stomachs. Like that they are more hygienic, he tells me. Then, he cooks the snails in butter and garlic. *Délicieux!*

FROGS

If you see a Frenchman carrying a red piece of cloth, an

umbrella, a rolling pin and a basket, he is probably on the hunt for frogs. The frog is enticed by the red cloth, moves and the hunter bashes it on the head with the rolling pin. The frog jumps and the Frenchman catches it in the upside-down umbrella on its dazed descent! The French eat the legs, of course, which taste like chicken. This perhaps explains why our pet name for the French is 'frogs': the name apparently stuck when English soldiers in France learnt about this French custom. In the same way, the French often call the British *les rosbifs,* because we are known for eating roast beef.

AT THE SEA SHORE

I have witnessed the same trait of foraging in the French character at the seaside, too, very early in the morning at low tide; carrier bags being replaced by buckets. In the south-west of France, on the Atlantic coast, they collect *palourdes* or clams. There is obviously a technique: I have seen grandfathers explaining it to their grandchildren. You stamp on the sand and the clams make their presence known by shooting up a jet of water. Then you rake the sand to collect them. In Corsica, the locals collect sea urchins, the soft inside of which is considered to be a delicacy.

TRADITIONS

The customs and traditions of what to collect, where and when are obviously handed down. I know adults whose haunts have been passed down by their grandparents. Naturally, this goes on to a greater extent in the countryside (or near the sea-side) than in the towns, but even my own young son in our small town is getting into the swing of things. He came home from school one day, pockets crammed with fresh figs: his sports teacher had spotted a tree in full fruit whilst they were at the local running track and he had encouraged the children to stock up because they are so full of goodness. My son said that although he had not forgotten my golden rule that he should never pick anything up off the ground, and very definitely should never eat anything he had found, his teacher's enthusiasm had got the better of him!

IT IS THE TASTE

The importance the French give to freshness probably explains why they are always on the lookout for nature's treasures. Picking dandelion leaves at just the right time ensures that you will eat them when they are at their best.

IT IS FREE

Another reason why the French pick anything that is good to eat is because of the satisfaction of getting something for nothing. There is no doubt either of the interest and admiration that is bestowed on that Frenchman when he shares his find at mealtime with his friends and family: his adventure becomes the main topic of conversation.

But for whatever reason the French cling to their traditional practices and customs of collecting and gathering, one thing is certain, they are fascinating to a foreigner like me. Anyone for nettle soup?

24
Le vide-grenier

I know that spring has arrived once more, and it is not only the new shoots on the vines that tell me so: it is the wealth of posters for *vide-greniers* – local second-hand sales – that herald the coming of the warm weather. Literally, this is the season for emptying attics or spare rooms cluttered with unwanted objects. The organisers are often local sports clubs, schools or groups of residents in the area, aiming to either raise funds or simply create some community spirit.

When I first arrived in France, this sort of *brocante* (second-hand market) for ordinary folk, fascinated me and I spent many a mild Sunday morning wandering round, bargain hunting and keeping my eyes open for French knick-knacks like Limoges pottery and *fèves* (good-luck charms that they add to their *Galette des Rois* cakes in January). But since then – encouraged by my French friends and neighbours – I have actually taken part in a number of annual *vide-greniers* organised in my area.

A GOOD REASON FOR A CLEAROUT

Why, one may ask, do I pay for the use of a couple of metres of space in a school playground or in a village square only to stand around all day in the hope of – more or less – giving away my unwanted possessions? One of the reasons is that from time to time my home, like those of my fellow stallholders, seems to become weighed down with objects I no longer use and the sale provides an opportunity to let go of these things. Naturally, there is no question of getting rid of those things with any sentimental attachment and there is even less point in trying to prise objects from my husband or children at the risk of them forever holding it against me!

EARNING A MODEST SUM

Another reason why being a *brocanteur d'un jour* has its attraction, of course, is that you can actually earn a modest sum of euros. (In fact officially you are limited to doing only a certain small number a year.) With the prospect of financing a day out for the family, buying a birthday present or a meal in a restaurant, even my children have been encouraged to have a look around their bedrooms for things that they could do without. In this way, too, they have become partners in an experience in which they have contributed as an equal. Not only has it been a test of their mental arithmetic, but the whole adventure has also enabled them to evaluate the cost and value of things.

FUN

Most importantly, however, the local *vide-grenier* is fun. My children and I have memories that I know we will giggle at for years to come. Highly recommended is that you undertake this adventure in a group since, if for nothing else, it avoids transporting everything alone and gives you a little free time at some point during the day of the sale.

For the newly-arrived in an area, the *vide-grenier* is an opportunity to get acquainted with new neighbours and to learn local habits. Round here at least, for the cost of the seven euros for two metres, the organisers throw in a free *apéritif* at midday which loosens any inhibitions you may have had up to that point!

PARLEZ-VOUS?

Above all, this particular day out has always been for me a chance to get to grips with one of the most daunting aspects of living abroad – the language. It often seems *so* much easier to let someone else speak English to us! Even when we do manage to master the basics, it is difficult to break through the 'intermediate' level. For those who are really determined about speaking their newly adopted language, local occasions like the *vide-grenier* maximise the opportunities of doing so. You feel less touchy about making mistakes and being corrected. Language is a living thing and get-togethers like this are moments of pure communication through visiting other stands and chatting with those nearby.

Tips

As for tips on getting the best out of the day, my neighbours have shared quite a few with me.

- They strongly recommend preparing for a *vide-grenier* a few weeks in advance in order to give yourself time to put aside the items you wish to sell: clothes, pots and pans, books – keeping in mind that everything and anything can be sold.

- Reserve your spot as soon as you can, although you will need to know how many metres to book. Two metres is the minimum. You may be tempted to reserve too many metres though: keep within your budget.

- For the big day – or *le jour 'j'* as the French say – you will need a vehicle sufficiently large to transport your things – and your display table or blanket since these are not always provided.

- Also take along sandwiches, drinks, and protection from the cold, the wind, the rain and the sun.

- Do not forget the necessary tools: bags, scissors, sticky tape, paper and markers. You will need lots of small change to carry on you of course.

- Finding a couple of friends to share your stand will not only be more fun but, so I am told, a well-stocked stand attracts more customers.

- In order to really make the most of your display, take along some cardboard boxes of different sizes to create some highlights and height on your exhibition table.

- Some stallholders attach a fine string across their table and hang objects or messages along it.

- Some even create a kids' corner of soft toys, jigsaw puzzles, comic books and magazines.

Finally, be prepared for the disappointment of selling too little. But as other *brocanteurs* will say, *'Ce n'est pas grave'*: the day was fun, you have fewer unwanted objects cluttering the house, you have met the new neighbours and the bit of cash that you have earned will not go wasted.

25
Observing and learning from *les femmes françaises*

When I first moved to France a passing comment in the *électroménager* department (household appliances) of the local supermarket, has forever coloured my views on French women.

I needed to buy a washing machine but the rows of them on offer gave me little choice. 'Why are most of these washing machines top-loaders? I have always had a front-loader,' I asked the assistant. '*Madame*,' she replied, 'Very few French women would actually choose to bend down to load their machines! Think of the extra effort. Also, when we forget to put in that odd sock, we can simply switch off a top-loader whilst, once the water is in a front-loader, that's it until the end of the programme.' Then the assistant paused, looked me in the eye and added, 'We French women always take the easy option whenever we can, *Madame*,' and as far as I am concerned, no truer word has ever been spoken.

STRESS-FREE DINING

The more I have observed *les femmes françaises* and their tendency to go for the stress-free solution, the more my admiration for them has grown. Take their attitude to entertaining. We British and American hostesses pride ourselves on our home-made cakes and desserts, willingly spending hours on purchasing the ingredients and baking them in our belief that the title Homemaker demands it of us. True, the French housewife may produce something from scratch, but there is not the same taboo surrounding a bought cake or dessert. Women here tend to serve their purchased *religieuses* and *mille-feuilles* on their *Limoges porcelaine* with pride at tea time and boast that they have found the best *pâtisserie* in town. I have known many a *dame* invite guests to dinner and openly admit that she has not made a thing herself. She meanwhile sits immaculately coiffured at the top of the table, which she has set beautifully at her leisure: forget slaving over a hot stove! She knows that given the importance of fresh, quality food to the French, she can talk at length of exactly where along the coast-line the oysters that they are eating are from, the ingredients with which the local *traiteur* made the main course and the location of the woods where the stallholder at the market picked the wild raspberries. There is no stress, no worry – and this is where you have to hand it to them – they know that the end result is far better than they could have managed on their own!

FINDING QUALITY TIME FOR THEMSELVES

There are numerous options available for child care at prices and in conditions rigorously supervised by the state.

Even mothers who do not work may leave their children from a very young age with professionals in the knowledge that it is an excellent way of familiarising youngsters to an environment different from that at home. *La halte-garderie* is available to children from three months to six years old on an occasional basis, from a few hours to a few half days a week. The flexible hours – whenever or for however long you need to leave your child – provides an opportunity for many mothers to pursue their own interests. There have been times when I have felt positively revitalised after these odd breaks from my toddlers during the week – and more importantly – better prepared to engage in constructive activity with them.

NO RUSHING

Many mothers opt for the *Crèche Municipale* which is available to children from two and a half months old to three years old for about eleven hours a day. Working mothers that I know do not seem to rush around at the end of the day in order to collect their child as soon as they leave work: they are confident about the care their child is receiving and do not feel guilty – they feel rather that they are entitled to some personal time.

A HOME FROM HOME

Some French mothers prefer to leave their children with an approved, registered child minder, an *Assistante Maternelle Agréée*, at her home full time. I have a number of friends who avoid stress all round in the mornings because they take their children to the child minder and then go back home to get ready for work.

147

Their *nounou* (the child's word for child-minder) often becomes something of a surrogate aunt or grand-mother and their house is considered to be a home from home. I have girl-friends who leave their children *chez la nounou* when they occasionally go away for an adult weekend with their husbands and everyone concerned is comfortable with the situation: these mums are not at a loss about what to do with their children and there is certainly no sense of guilt for leaving them with others for the weekend.

In the same way that mothers – both working and non-working – take advantage of the good child-care facilities offered by the state, where amenities are available and suited to the family, many mothers enrol their child at *l'école maternelle* from the age of two onwards. Very often, this is only for certain mornings, for example, and not all day and every day. A very young age for some, maybe, but these French mothers believe that through contact with adults and other children, their child has the opportunity of developing their language and view of the world.

LOOKING GOOD

This ability by French women of not allowing themselves to be totally consumed by their role as mother is one of the reasons why so many of them are so beautifully turned out. I was once chastised in a *salon de beauté* for 'neglecting' myself because – judging by my dry skin – it was felt by the staff that I had not taken enough time every day to moisturise. The fact that I had a couple of demanding toddlers, was no excuse I was told.

JUST WHAT THE DOCTOR ORDERED

From what I have seen, French women do not tend to turn their entire house into a play zone either. My children's paediatrician was always referring to this need for children to know their boundaries, and French women seem to adhere to this. The grants that families receive for having children are strictly based on regular medical visits when doctors insist on establishing routine and define clearly what is best for the child and for the whole family.

French women come in all shapes and sizes – very much as they do everywhere else. In general though, one thing they do not do is just 'soldier on'. What they do possess is *savoir-faire*: the know-how to achieve a good quality of life for themselves and for those around them.

26
The strip-cartoon

Supermarkets in France have one extensive aisle that always seems to draw plenty of interest – that of *la bande dessinée* or strip cartoon albums or graphic novels. There are volumes of them, the majority of a French-Belgian flavour: *Tintin, Gaston, Titeuf* to name but a few. France is a nation of *BD* lovers, as *bande dessinée* is commonly referred to over here.

HUGE INTEREST

Astérix, the comic-strip Gaulois heroes created by Goscinny and Uderzo in 1959, sells 3,500 to 4,000 of each of its titles a month. In view of such public demand, Hachette, the publishers have decided to give the first eight adventures a new look, including new covers and new colours. The comic strip has even inspired *Parc Astérix*, the popular theme park 30 kilometres north of Paris, which celebrated its 15th birthday in 2004. A stroll along *Via Antiqua* reveals architecture and souvenirs from *Astérix*'s journeys, while the *Astérix* Village and Roman camp are reconstructions from the cartoons.

NOT JUST KIDS' STUFF

How wrong I was to assume that the followers of the *bande dessinée* were only the younger generation. Naturally, children read them and *BD* albums seem to be the standard birthday gift at parties. I remember when eight of my son's invited friends arrived in turn, each one of them bearing an adventure of *Spirou* or *Cédric*.

SERIOUS READING MATTER

My own childhood memories of the stocking-filler Beano Album can be blamed for lulling me into the illusion that I knew what a comic strip album was! It came as some surprise to discover that French *BD* fans include a great number of adults as well as children. I blush to think that I once made the terrible *faux-pas* of laughing at a middle-aged man when he proudly told me about his vast collection of *'Les Adventures de Blake et Mortimer'*. These hardback copies are full-length stories which are as much about science and history as pure escapism. They are educational with settings in far away places like Egypt and Mexico and far off times like pre-history. Go into any FNAC or large bookshop and sensible and serious people of all ages will be propping up the shelves, devouring the album they are reading; attracted by the colourful designs, unable to put it down until they get to the end of the gripping storyline.

HOMAGE TO THE GRAND MASTERS

The *Festival International de la Bande Dessinée d'Augoulême* takes place every year and 2006 saw its 33rd year, attracting young and old, amateur and professional collectors alike. The *Centre National de la Bande Dessinée et d'Image* – also in Angoulême – pays homage to the Grand Masters of the strip cartoon. It houses almost all of French strip cartoon production from 1946 onwards and its large stock of material (video cassettes, cartoon albums, magazines and so on) may be freely consulted. The *Centre* has recently become the new home to the complete collection of Marvel comics, which include the superheroes Spiderman and X-Men.

In its ambitions to satisfy *BD* audiences all year round, the *festival* has even reached its tentacles to the capital – to the prestigious surroundings of the *Musée de l'Homme* in Paris. It devoted an exhibition to Edgar P. Jacobs and his characters Blake and Mortimer in 2004, marking Jacob's 100th anniversary. The exhibition honoured the man – often considered a visionary – who is one of the principal icons of the European strip cartoon world. The exhibition drew on the favourite images of the stories of the two English detectives, which first appeared in 1946 in Belgium. It was organised by theme in 19 rooms, covering a total of 1,000 square metres. Further evoking the atmosphere and décor of the series, the *Musée de l'Homme* contributed Egyptian artefacts, Indian totem poles, tiger skulls and even 1950s electric machines.

THE *MANGA* MANIA

Younger *bande dessinée* fans have been particularly hooked on the Japanese inspired *manga* mania. *Manga* is a *BD* in black and white, which you read from right to left. A Japanese person would take about 20 minutes to read the 320 pages of a *manga* – a time that corresponds to the commute from work to home.

These stories are published on recycled paper and once finished with are thrown into special waste bins.

Here in France, the *manga* was not actually received with open arms by parents at first, even though they themselves may well have been brought up reading *BDs*. In the 1980s, the children's show *'Club Dorothée'* first showed the Japanese animated cartoons like *'Goldorak', 'Albator'* and *'Chevaliers du Zodiaque'* which exasperated parents. At the time, parents considered these cartoons violent and consequently the *manga* had a bad press. Directors of children's programmes today closely regulate these series before they appear on the screen so that fewer parents worry about the time and pocket money their children spend on *mangas*.

Hot off the press

Nowadays, it is a common sight in bookshops to see recently delivered *mangas* – not even on the shelves – being sold to queues of youngsters already lining up at the counter. They know – thanks to the Internet – that a new adventure of their favourite hero has just come out in French. Fans have been known to even buy the Japanese version without being able to speak a word of the language itself just in order to get to know the end of the story before their friends.

The reason why ten- to 15-year-olds are seduced by heroes answering to puzzling names like Naruto, Yuyu Hashusho, Sakura, Imakodi, Kimengumi is that the reader finds in them stories that mirror their own problems: themes like love and bravery. In Japan the production of the *manga* is vast and segmented. There are *mangas* for 4- to 6-year-olds, for 6- to 8-year-old boys, for housewives, university students, bachelors, and so on. It is a powerful industry that employs hundreds of authors and publishes several millions of copies every week.

What is particularly appealing though, is that in the Japanese culture the distinction between good and bad is not as clear-cut as in our own. The goodies are not all good and the baddies are not all bad and teenagers like this absence of stereotypes. Thanks to their magic powers, the characters might seem like Spiderman or Superman but they are not model heroes. They do not evolve in a rigid manner and graphically nearly anything is possible.

It is true that not every Frenchman would elevate the strip cartoon to the heights of great literature. Nevertheless, *Le Figaro Magazine* serialised the original 1948 version of *'Tintin au pays de l'or noir'* throughout the summer months in 2004, which just goes to show the high esteem in which the *BD* is held as reading matter.

27
Sport and the younger generation

Parents all over France have one thing on their minds as the summer months close and September approaches: *la rentrée*, or the run up to the beginning of the new school year. Supermarkets are packed with mums and dads clutching school lists of required materials in one hand while at the same time piling exercise books, writing paper, paints and so on into their *chariots* – and here the French word for 'supermarket trolley' aptly sets the scene.

Once that hurdle is over however, there is yet another mission for parents to complete: a sporting activity needs to be chosen, for – as anyone who lives with the French soon realises – they believe that in addition to eating well, physical activity is good for your health.

WEDNESDAY AFTERNOON

Judging by the amount of sport going on around me in the small provincial town where I live, much of it takes place in clubs and associations outside school grounds and out of school time.

Once a year there is a large forum where families can go from stand to stand in an attempt to get the choice down to one or two, the options available are so numerous. In fact, one of the reasons why children do not have school on Wednesday afternoon is to enable them to take up an activity that is not on the school curriculum.

Not too young

There seems to be a unanimous agreement amongst my French friends that it is not a good idea to introduce a child too early to a sport, however. Apart from swimming and gym, the age of six to seven is the best time to start because that is about the time when a child has some degree of coordination.

The child's choice

Local clubs themselves advise parents not to decide on a sport without the agreement of their child because otherwise the child may abandon the activity very quickly. They say that the main thing is that a child should be enjoying his sport.

Spoilt for choice

There is not only a wealth of choice of sports at local clubs and associations but they offer a wide range of times after school and at weekend. Classes aimed at differing levels of competence are available too. Parents seem to go about their choice in a fairly systematic manner and they generally match the physical activity with the type of child they have.

- When a child likes to perform, an individual sport – like judo or gym – is appropriate.

- On the other hand, if they like the idea of being in opposition to others, a collective sport – like rugby, handball or football – might suit well.

- If they are not sporty by nature, pony riding, for example, might be fun.

- For those children who need to channel their energy, more physical disciplines – like athletics or swimming – may be best.

- A shy child could have a go at judo in order to build up confidence.

No girl–boy boundary

As for certain sports only for girls and certain sports only for boys, it is – I am told – really a question of character and physique since nowadays, girls can feel totally comfortable in sports that used to be the reserve of boys only, such as football.

Properly qualified coaching

We often hear of some sports not being adapted to everyone because of problems of health. I always thought that children with back problems, for example, should avoid particular sports. Some parents avoid contact sports, like rugby, for their children fearing that – despite it being a sport that develops a real sense of team spirit – it is a sport in which their child may risk more injury than in others. However, the general feeling seems to be that, whatever sport it is, as long as the trainer or coach is properly qualified, children risk very little from the point of view of their well being.

Cost

On average, the cost of enrolling a child in a club for a year, including the equipment and the insurance fee, varies from around 100 up to 150 euros. A number of sports involve extremely expensive equipment and not all parents can afford this. Others do not want to run the risk of wasting money if the child abandons the sport when it is no longer any fun, especially when – as is sometimes the case – the child has been inspired to take up the sport in the first place having watched a television programme!

A cheaper option

Parents do have a less expensive option open to them. At a cost of about 20 euros a year, they can enrol their child in sessions organised by the school. These sessions are called *l'USEP* for primary school children and *l'UNSS* for children of secondary school age.

These sporting activities and competitions organised by the school are run by the teachers themselves and have the support of the parents' associations. They are considered to be an extension of the compulsory physical education that children already have on their school timetables.

TIMETABLED SPORT AT SCHOOL

The number of taught PE lessons varies according to the age of the children: three or four hours a week. The interesting point is that even the most senior pupils – no matter whether they are studying the sciences or the arts – have compulsory sport that counts towards their final *baccalauréat* (high school diploma) and this seems to reflect the importance of physical education to the public at large.

THE IMPORTANCE OF SPORT

It is true that the French are as concerned by the growing obesity amongst young people as anyone else and that probably explains why they are so keen for their children to take part in sports both in and out of school time. They say that it instils some discipline and forces children to be good timekeepers. Collective sports are excellent, they argue because they teach children how to work as part of a team.

From a social point of view, too, the French enrol their children for skiing trips, initiation classes at the local golf club as well as week-long beginners' courses at the tennis club because they do not want their children to feel 'left out' later on.

AN ACTIVE NATION

The French interest in fitness, though, is not simply a matter of parents encouraging their children to do a sport. They want their children to be like themselves: active on a regular basis. The provincial French person is one who moves! I see elderly people – no matter the season – walking to the local market and back. My Sunday afternoon cycle ride along our local river banks can be a struggle at times with families – pushchairs, wheelchairs and all – every 50 metres all out for a stroll along the path, as well as the amateur fishermen and all their paraphernalia! I notice people of all ages foraging in the fields and woods, wandering about in the countryside or on the beaches clutching their finds. It is not just the food they are looking for, nor simply the fresh air: I think they like being active and they know that it is good for them.

28
The local festival

Imagine the scene. It is early evening in a small town in the south west of France. It could be any dark, cold, wet November night. There is the odd man propping up a local bar. Otherwise, there is no one around. Shutters are firmly closed, the place is extremely quiet … and you ask yourself how France gets its reputation for the good life.

A VERITABLE TRANSFORMATION

Visit the same town over five days and five nights in the last week of July and the French *joie de vivre* is only too evident. Every shade of the blues – be it gospel, soul, rhythm'n blues, Chicago blues, Delta blues – reverberates in the town from early morning until sunset. It is almost impossible *not* to come across some musician or other. This very transformation takes place every year to an ever growing public. It is the *Cognac Blues Passions* festival. The French know how to do festivals and this one is a ball.

We are not talking here about a village fête – in recent years, the festival has attracted about 40,000 festival-goers. Previous *Cognac Blues Passions* have witnessed prestigious artists like

BB King, Ray Charles, Taj Mahal, Bill Wyman and The Rhythm Kings ... some of whom have never actually played in France before. But the objective of the festival is for the public to discover young – and French – talent too.

EVERYONE IS WELCOME

Apart from the quality of the music, another reason for the popularity of the festival is that it is accessible to everyone. In past years, there have been 66 programmed concerts of which 53 were *free*. Put another way, *Cognac Blues Passions* means five days of more or less non-stop music, for nothing!

The principle of dividing the concert throughout the town is that it enables the public to find exactly the type of blues they are looking for – from funk to gospel – at whatever time of the day they prefer. It might be *petit déjeuner* (*café* and *croissants* available) in the public gardens with the Bernie'Jazz Band, a pre-lunch *apéritif* with the Brasshoppers or an afternoon *goûter* with Aynsley Lister.

Spreading the fun around allows everyone to get a look in, from children to the elderly as well as summer tourists stopping off in town for a couple of hours on the way to the coast. The atmosphere is *sympa*: you do not need to be 'knowledgeable' about the blues to participate.

Every evening, the blues resound in 11 bars in the town – including the one at the campsite – with free live music from nine o'clock in the evening, often until two o'clock in the early morning during the four evenings of the festival. The choice is between nursing a drink all night in the same bar or experiencing an unforgettable pub-crawl!

THE SETTING

The epicentre of the *Cognac Blues Passions* festival is the beautiful public garden, *l'Hotel de Ville*. It was here that, during a terrible hurricane in December 1999, 237 of its 600 trees were destroyed. The garden has since been re-designed and trees have been replanted. It is an idyllic venue – a friendly, welcoming one in which you can come and go, sit on the grass or under a tree while you listen. The weather helps of course because, although no one can promise wall-to-wall sunshine, given that the festival takes place in late July, there is a good chance of it.

Some of the other settings for the ticket paying concerts are magical too. The afternoon 'River Blues' is an acoustic cruise along the local Mississippi – *la Charente*. 'The Groove *au Château*' takes place in the guards' room of the Renaissance château where Francis 1st King of France was born.

A FRIENDLY ATMOSPHERE

A certain intimacy between the musicians and their public has characterised the previous *Cognac Blues Passions* festivals. My neighbour still raves about Ike Turner (yes, Tina's ex) whom he swears only looked about 50 even though he was 71 at the time. A special showing of Ray – the film – was shown at the local cinema when Ray Charles died, so deeply was his loss felt by the locals who had been touched that such a great celebrity had graced their festival a few years previously. Whereas no doubt at more commercial concerts, you cannot get near the musicians, here the whole family get close up along with holiday makers and the serious fans.

The musicians evidently feel the friendly atmosphere too. A local taxi driver recounted at length how two of the singers of The Blind Boys of Alabama (the legendary gospel group made up of seven musicians) got down off the stage with their microphones. Apparently, to the delight of the audience who went delirious – the taxi-driver included.

THE COST

As for the running costs, although in 2002, there were 120 voluntary helpers who were divided into nine groups, they worked side by side with professional organisers. A good dozen sound engineers with the same number of lighting technicians produce an installation capable of spitting out about 90,000 watts! How can a local festival which cost about 520,000 euros one year put on such an event? The answer is that some of the cost is covered by grants, some by sponsorship and some tickets.

IT IS GOOD FOR THE ECONOMY OF THE TOWN

There is the belief that the *Cognac Blues Passions* festival reaps benefits for the town. Hotels, restaurants and bars naturally see more visitors than at more sleepy times of the year, but local people, too, are encouraged to let out their spare rooms.

The intention is also that visitors become acquainted with both *cognac* – the drink – the world famous 'king of brandies', an elegant spirit distilled from wine and Cognac, the town itself – a place whose people and surrounding countryside produce this noble *eau-de-vie*.

Cognac is produced exclusively in two small *départments* in the southwest of France, Charente and Charente-Maritime, in a strictly limited area. Every stage in the making of *cognac* is exclusively local (and subject to extremely stringent rules and regulations). The grapes are grown there; the wine is distilled in traditional pot stills manufactured in the region. The barrels for ageing *cognac* are hand-crafted in local cooperages from wood grown in nearby forests. Even the bottles are produced at a factory in the town.

It is worth keeping an eye open for festivals in even small French towns – and not just during the summer months – because the locals generally throw their heart and soul into them. As far as the *Cognac Blues Passions* is concerned, the alchemy that transforms the local grapes into 'the nectar of the gods' is very like the transformation of the town during those five days and nights when it becomes the host for what is arguably one of the top blues festivals in Europe.

29
La vendange with a difference

When I was living in the UK, I remember toasting the year's grape harvest over a glass of *Beaujolais Nouveau*. Since I have been living amongst the vines myself here in south-west France, my family and I have celebrated many a wine harvest with the locals during a weekend's *Fête de la Vendange*. We have watched barrel rolling competitions, floats of young girls and women in their customary *quichenotte* (kiss-me-not) headdresses and we have eaten the same traditional dishes that grape-pickers of yesteryear ate.

PAMPERED IN VINE EXTRACTS

Last year was different, though – and very special – because I spent *la vendange* in paradise. To be more exact, while my husband and children were wandering around the little French village of Martillac in the middle of the *Grave* vineyards south of Bordeaux, I was being pampered with beauty treatments based on vine and grape extracts at the elegant *Caudalie Vinothérapie Spa*. I include this episode here because it exemplifies the extent to which the French take seriously both the frivolous and the serious in life, and this is one of the reasons why France is such a wonderful place to bring up a family.

A NATURAL SPA

This is the French art of living at its finest. The Spa is a natural thermal source and a luxurious centre for body care. Next door is its exclusive hotel *Les Sources de Caudalie* in which every single suite and room has a unique character and where there are two gastronomic restaurants – one of which is a one-star Michelin. All this is in a setting of 130 acres of picturesque vines with a view of the 16th century tower of the Château Smith Haut Lafitte estate, housing cellars of red and white wine of great vintages.

The estate's history goes back to the Crusades. A Scottish navigator, George Smith, became the owner in the 18th century. Large quantities of his wine were exported to England, gaining him an international reputation. Florence and Daniel Cathiard purchased the Château in 1990 and their passion for vines and their traditions led to a spectacular upturn for the label. Wine buffs know all about the sensation their award-winning wines have caused.

A DISCARDED TREASURE

Not long after the Cathiards bought Château Smith Haut Lafitte, during the grape harvest of 1993, their eldest daughter Mathilde and her husband were out walking around the old *grand cru* estate with Professor Vercauteren, a researcher at *La Faculté de Pharmacie de Bordeaux*. When they came across a bin full of discarded grape seeds, the professor pointed out that they were throwing away a real treasure. He went on to explain that the polyphenols concentrated in grapes contain anti-oxidants capable of effectively combating free radicals and their agents – smoke, stress, pollution – which are among the chief suspects in ageing skin. According to his studies, grape-seed oil slows down the skin's ageing process and is rich in fatty acids so is therefore an ideal nutrient for softening and moisturizing the skin.

In September 1995, Mathilde launched a grape-seed-oil infused skin-care line called *Caudalie* – named after the unit of measure oenologists use to describe how long a particular wine lingers on the palate. The whole secret of the patent rests on the stabilisation of grape polyphenols and The Claudalie Laboratories benefit from years of research done by the team at Bordeaux. The success of her effective Caudalie cosmetics line based on essential extracts derived from grapes inspired her to develop a pioneering range of therapies. In 1999 the Cathiards opened the hotel and spa, *Les Sources de Caudalie*.

VINOTHERAPHY

At the spa, excess weight, wrinkles and cellulite are treated with the unique vinotheraphy techniques – using the discards of winemaking for the benefits of the body. In the Wine Barrel Bath, you can soak in bubbling hot spring water drawn up from 540 metres below the estate, plus fresh, finely-crushed grape extracts from seed, skin, stalk and pulp. A Crushed Cabernet Scrub may be the perfect start to your treatments to rid your skin of dead cells. There is the Sauvignon Massage available, using grape-seed oil from Sauvignon grapes. I personally, experienced the Pulp Friction Massage (which is only available during the grape harvest) – a full body treatment – the benefits of which are to restore a clear, soft and moisturised skin. A wide range of treatments is available depending on the results you want and there is a medical team available to clients on request. The Spa offers a programme of exclusive treatments in a beautiful environment surrounded by vineyards.

PURIFICATION OR PLEASURE

You *can* pre-order special 500-calorie meals. During the harvest, a purification programme is offered that calls for eating only grapes, lasting anything from one to seven days. The treatment draws the toxins out of the body and works on the liver, intestines, kidneys and waistline.

But this is France! Clients come to unwind, to take better care of themselves and to relax. With pleasure in mind, the restaurants have two different approaches. One of them is the Michelin-starred 'La Grand Vigne'. Its terrace, overlooking a pond at the foot of a vine-covered slope, was inspired by 18th century orangeries. The chef incorporates unusual ingredients into classic French dishes.

The other restaurant is 'La Table du Lavoir' which serves stylish country food in an informal atmosphere. It is housed on the site of a charming old washhouse where grape-pickers used to beat their laundry.

AWARD-WINNING WINES

Naturally, *Les Sources de Caudalie* goes hand in hand with

quality wines. The sommelier is responsible for a cellar of 15,000 bottles, amongst which star the red and white wines of the hotel's own Château Smith Haut Lafitte wines, a *cru classé* Graves.

During their stay at the hotel and between sessions at the spa, visitors can taste the most famous Bordeaux wines by the glass at the bar. At 'La Tour aux Cigares' with its magnificent view of the Château, they can relax with a fine *cognac* and a Havana. For those guests really wanting to take advantage of the countryside, they can bike through the vineyards and forests, or tour the wine cellars of the famous Bordeaux wine region.

The bar at *Les Sources de Caudalie* is called 'Le French Paradox.' It is thanks to the French that it is widely accepted nowadays that a glass or two of wine a day is good for you. What is apparent also is that the secrets of the grape are found not just in the glass but in its skin and seeds too.

30
Festivities that focus on food and drink

I used to think that I only needed to blink and I would miss Christmas in our sleepy little town. People do not send each other Christmas cards, nor do they stand around the piano singing Christmas carols and, since religion (and politics) are strictly off the school curriculum, my children have never invited me to a school nativity play of any sort. There seemed to be no festive spirit. I realise now, though, that the French just do things differently.

FORGET THE CHRISTMAS CARDS

Take greetings cards. The French do wish every health and happiness to their friends, family and acquaintances, but this is not done before the 25th December and it is not done via a Christmas card.

Their *cartes de vœux* are sent at the beginning of the New Year. You would not be snubbing a friend either if you did not send a card because often the French do not actually send one – they phone their friends expressly to pass on their greetings. The

French give themselves until the last day of January to exchange their wishes for the New Year in this way.

As for people they see everyday, an opportunity will be found to wish one another '*Bonne année, bonne santé et mes meilleurs vœux*' and with these words, they shake hands or kiss cheeks even more enthusiastically than usual. This exchange is a must the first day back at work after the Christmas holidays and you may as well set half the morning aside because it would be a real slight not to extend your greetings to a colleague or acquaintance.

COMPLIMENTS OF THE SEASON

There were a number of Christmas customs that I did not even recognised as such when I first arrived in France. One December morning, my postman rang my doorbell to ask if I wanted to buy a calendar. I said 'No thank you' but I knew instinctively from the disappointment on his face and his quick getaway that I had made a blunder.

My neighbour explained that I really *did* need to buy his calendar. You see it is the one time in the year when you can express your gratitude to your postman for doing his job efficiently (if that is the case). In other words, instead of simply wishing 'Compliments of the Season' in the hope of getting a tip, selling a calendar is their more elegant way of getting one. The firemen and the dustbin-men also come a-knocking with their calendars during the month of December.

WHEN *UN ARBRE* IS NOT A TREE

With the absence of Christmas celebrations at school, I assumed that my children would just have to get used to life without a Christmas party. Then one December, we were invited to an *Arbre de Noël* ('a Christmas Tree'). In total confusion, I asked around if this meant that we were invited to *buy* a Christmas tree. No, my friends insisted, we were invited *to* a Christmas tree. I asked if we were going to *see* a Christmas tree. Well, perhaps we might be able to do that, they answered.

In fact, *un Arbre de Noël* is a Christmas party for all the children whose parents work together. In some firms, it is the owner who throws the party and sometimes it is the works' committee. Father Christmas gives each child a present and there is sometimes a magician or a clown who provides the entertainment.

FOOD GLORIOUS FOOD

But the point is that given the French love of food and given how they particularly enjoy long drawn-out family occasions, it seems to me that the important element for them at Christmas time is *the meal* itself. Traditionally, this used to be eaten on Christmas Eve after mass at around midnight. After mass because Catholics do not eat before they have taken communion. Nowadays, most people seem to have their meal at midday on the 25th (whether they go to mass or not).

The Christmas meal itself consists of all the fine wines and food we associate with the French. They would have already stocked up on champagne and wine for the festive season during the

Foire au Vins (promotional wine week) in the supermarkets and specialist wine shops in the autumn.

Oyster tents are erected outside supermarkets a few days before the 25th for shoppers to purchase their starter course. I peep into these tents to see wooden boxes piled up according to category. Personally, I am overcome by the choice. It is not only the size and shape of the shell that matter but also whether you prefer them milky or green. I ask my friends how they keep what are, after all, live shellfish fresh until they are eaten. Surely a fridge would not hold a large wooden box like that. *Pas de problème*, they keep them unpacked in their boxes in the garage or cellar where it is cold enough for the oysters to stay fresh for about eight days. Keeping them in a fridge would be too cold for the oysters, which must always be eaten live.

Fois gras comes next on the menu. This is a smooth rich paste made from the liver of a specially fattened goose and is considered to be a great delicacy. Again, the choice is enormous and you have to educate yourself first on what is what. I used to presume that *fois gras* that came in tins and was always second-rate, but I have been put right by many a fellow-shopper! I have some friends who will actually go and collect their *fois gras* from their favourite producer.

Turkey or goose seems to be the preferred meat for the main course stuffed with cooked chestnuts (*marrons*) – and, once again, do not turn your nose up at the tinned variety which may be considered the most tasty.

Le plateau de fromages and fresh green salad follows and, as a rule of thumb, regional favourite cheeses will usually take precedent over any gimmicky unknown.

NO *GÂTEAUX DE NOËL*

Forget the Christmas cake and the Christmas pudding because whilst the French often serve the traditional Christmas Log (*Bûche de Noël*) for dessert, the cake they associate with this time of year is the *Galette des Rois*. The *galette* (the kings' cake) is not eaten at Christmas at all but in the New Year. It celebrates Epiphany, which is on the 6th January and marks the arrival of the three wise men to rejoice in the birth of Christ with their gifts.

I am far from being an advocate of over-the-top Christmas commercialisation at the beginning of November or Santa's grotto with its high-energy consumption in every front garden. Nevertheless, it has taken me some time to get used to the relatively low-key build up to Christmas in France. Nowadays, I can actually see the French point of view – decorations and gifts are all very well but the good life is eating fine food and drinking fine wines with the people you love, *n'est-ce pas?*

31
The *Galette des Rois*

Given the French reputation for good food, it is hardly surprising that a cake will be the given excuse for many a party over the weeks following the Christmas celebrations. At work, colleagues will share it over a glass of cider; children will eat it after a game together at their local sports club or music class and hostesses everywhere will serve it at their dinner parties with champagne. It is the *Galette des Rois* (the kings' cake).

DIFFERENT RECIPES

Although the *galette* is always round in shape, there is a choice of recipes. The most delicious – in my opinion – is the one based on pastry flavoured with ground almonds or *frangipane* (see the recipe below). But the *Galette des Rois* can also be a large circular *brioche* with a hole in the centre made with the very best butter and fresh eggs and studded with glacé cherries and angelica.

Over the past couple of years the range has even extended to apple *compôte* being added to the *frangipane* and chocolate chips replacing the glacé cherries. But whatever type of cake, there is one thing that accompanies the festivity – a crown. It is precisely the ceremony of who gets to wear the crown that makes the eating of the *Galette des Rois* such fun.

THE CHARM

Bakers add a lucky charm whenever they make a *galette*. The lucky one who finds the charm in their piece of cake gets to choose who becomes *le roi* or *la reine*.

This custom of putting a charm in the *galette*, is very like our coin (or in the olden days a thimble or six-penny piece) being stirred into our Christmas pudding. The *fève* – meaning lucky charm – used to mean that word literally: a broad bean bringing good luck to whoever found it. Nowadays, though, the lucky charm is usually a very small porcelain model or statuette. It might be an animal from the stable scene at Christ's birth. More often than not, it is a religious or fairy tale character or a craftsman. A national radio programme recently suggested that the most popular *fève* characters this year are likely to be those from the Harry Potter books!

I have French friends who have collected these lucky charms over the years from their childhood days. They are kept in small cabinets and have great sentimental value. *Fèves* even change hands at antique fairs and in second-hand shops.

Those who collect *des fève des rois* in my region have organised themselves into *l'association des fabophiles* and hold sales when they have the opportunity of exchanging whole series of *fèves* for another series. For them, the objective is not to make any money but to finance their collections. Individual *fèves* usually change hands for centimes but rare ones can fetch up to ten or 15 euros. Their sales draw other *fabophiles* from a dozen or so other regions of France and 120 metres of stands display their wares. Their catalogues for 2003 and 2004 list 5,000 different series of *fèves* and 6,200 for 2005.

THE FUN IS IN THE SERVING

The ritual of serving the *galette* whenever there are children involved, verges on the ceremonial. The important point is that the cake is given out fairly and that there is no favouritism. In order to achieve this, the youngest member of the family or group hides under the table whilst the *galette* is being cut and shared out. The child shouts out the name of the person to whom each piece should be given. One extra piece is traditionally left on the plate – this is the symbolic piece for absent friends.

The person who finds the *fève* in their piece of *galette* not only gets good luck throughout the year but is also given the honour of choosing the queen or her king from amongst those present. A coronation takes place and the king or queen wears the crown for the rest of the evening.

There is one other important tradition that accompanies the *Fête des Rois* – the person who found the *fève* has to buy another *galette*! So, although the *galette* celebrates Epiphany, which is on the 6th January and marks the arrival of the three wise men to rejoice in the birth of Christ with their gifts, the *Fête des Rois* in fact lasts throughout the month of January.

La Galette des Rois (for six people)

200g plain flour
100g ground almonds
100g castor sugar
100g butter, softened
3 egg yolks
1 pinch of salt
2 x 15 ml spoons rum or kirsch

Mix together the flour and ground almonds in a bowl.

Add the sugar, eggs, salt, rum or kirsch and butter.

Knead the ingredients together to form a ball.

Do not forget to add your lucky charm!

By hand, place the pastry into a 24cm diameter cake tin.

Flatten it evenly.

Brush the surface of the *galette* with egg yolk.

With a sharp knife, make shallow cuts to create a lattice design.

Bake in a moderately hot oven for about 25 minutes until golden brown.

Bonne Fête des Rois!

Appendix

USEFUL WEBSITES

Le Ministère de l'éducation
nationale de l'enseignement
supérieur et de la recherche   *www.education.gouv.fr*

Office national d'information sur les
enseignements et les professions   *www.onisep.fr*

Centre national d'enseignement
à distance   *www.cned.fr*

Centre d'information et de
documentation jeunesse   *www.cidj.asso.fr*

Universities and Colleges
Admissions Service   *www.ucas.com*

Angoulême BD festival   *www.bdangouleme.com*

Cognac Blues Passions   *www.bluespassions.com*

Les Sources de Caudalie   *www.sources-caudalie.com*

Don't get caught out when making regular foreign currency transfers

Even once you have bought your property in France you need to make sure that you don't forget about foreign exchange. It's highly likely that you'll need to make regular foreign currency transfers from the UK whether for mortgage payments, maintenance expenditure or transferring pensions or salaries, and you may not realise that using your bank to arrange these transfers isn't always the best option. Low exchange rates, high fees and commission charges all eat away at your money and mean that each time you use your bank you lose out. However, by using Currencies Direct's Overseas Regular Transfer Plan you can get more of your money time after time.

Exchange Rates
Your bank is likely to only offer you a tourist rate of exchange due to the small amounts being transferred. However, Currencies Direct is able to offer you a commercial rate of exchange regardless of the amount that you wish to transfer.

Transfer Charges
Most banks will typically charge between £10 and £40 for every monthly transfer. Currencies Direct is able to offer free transfers, which will save you a considerable amount of money over time.

Commission Charges
When made through a bank transfers are usually liable for a commission charge of around 2%. By using Currencies Direct you can avoid commission charges altogether.

How does it work?
It is very easy to use Currencies Direct. The first thing you need to do is open an account with them. Once this is done all you need to do is set up a direct debit with your bank and confirm with Currencies Direct how much money you would like to send and how often (monthly or quarterly). They will then take the money from your account on a specified day and once they have received the cleared funds transfer it to France at the best possible rate available.

Information provided by Currencies Direct.
Website: *www.currenciesdirect.com*
Email: *info@currenciesdirect.com*
Tel: 0845 389 1729

Index